EUROPEAN POLITICAL, ECONOMIC, AND SECURITY ISSUES

AN IN DEPTH LOOK AT HUNGARY

European Political, Economic, and Security Issues

Additional books and e-books in this series can be found on Nova's website under the Series tab.

EUROPEAN POLITICAL, ECONOMIC, AND SECURITY ISSUES

AN IN DEPTH LOOK AT HUNGARY

ESPERANTA ROMPA
EDITOR

nova
science publishers
New York

Additional color graphics may be available in the e-book version of this book.

Library of Congress Cataloging-in-Publication Data

ISBN: 978-1-53615-351-4

Published by Nova Science Publishers, Inc. † New York

Contents

PREFACE

An In Depth Look at Hungary opens with a chapter suggesting that socio-economic inequalities are one of the most relevant barriers to healthcare access in Hungary. Some mechanisms for decision-making are studied using content-analysis according to the Hungarian health policy strategies and concepts.

Next, this collection provides an overview of the Hungarian teacher education system, describing social and cultural features of the country as well the main parameters of the Hungarian education system.

The authors investigate the development of irregular armed forces comprised of local citizens which were deployed in border protection. Border protection has received increased attention in modern times, particularly regarding the mountain ranges which serve as a natural defensive zone when entering the country.

The concluding chapter demonstrates those instruments by which an excessively polarized society could be prevented in the near future.

Chapter 1 - There are numerous studies relating to health inequalities highlighting the role of access to health care. However this research is usually focussed on regional distribution of that care. Our case study made in Hungary is based on quantitative and qualitative examinations which describes the connection between health inequalities and barriers of accessibility. With this context in mind, this chapter aims to analyse the

Hungarian health inequalities in terms of space and time, after the political and economic transition of 1989, defining the influence of accessibility on those inequalities. Therefore this chapter contains three main structural parts, which aim to identify the theoretical background and empirical results with its primary conclusions, regarding Hungarian health inequalities and difficulties in accessing those services. Firstly, our aims and methods are clearly shown, to give an easier understanding of the scientific and empirical framework in our research. Additionally, the authors have strongly highlighted importantance of international and Hungarian preliminaries as very different approaches in defining the role of accessibility in health inequalities. Then, statistical analyses can help to discover how mortality rates and life expectancies have changed timely and spatially in Hungary in the last more than 25 years. The following section highlights the most informative experiences of the presented national and local case studies on examining primary barriers in access to health care. The unequal access to health care often varies according to the type of health service, which is the main reason that the case study is focusing on the area of infarction care through one of noncommunicable diseases such as acute myocardial infarction. Likewise, some local barriers and availabilities in access to infarction care are also explained. There are based on making on semi-structured interviews with health care stakeholders. Finally, some areas and mechanisms of decision-making are studied by content-analysis according to the Hungarian health policy strategies and concepts. The major conclusion of this chapter is that socio-economic inequalities are one of the most relevant barriers in access to health care which might leading to increased health inequalities.

Chapter 2 - The study aims to give an overview of the Hungarian teacher education system. The authors describe the social and cultural features of the country and the main parameters of the Hungarian education system (e.g., the relationship between social mobility and education). The authors try to give an adequate framework by which the system of teacher education can be interpreted. The presentation of the teacher education program includes a short historical overview. The Bologna Process and its subsequent modifications are also analyzed. Our aim is to describe the present features of different types of training programs and institutions. Teacher education students' socio-cultural background is also investigated. This is a very important issue because students from a disadvantaged background are generally overrepresented in teacher education. During the past fifteen years, several circumstances have changed in the system of teacher education (aptitude test, training set-up, the curriculum of training programs, special scholarship programs for students, teaching practice). The authors try to list these important changes and analyze their potential and direct effects.

Chapter 3 - Border protection received increased attention in early modern times; particularly the mountain ranges, which served as a natural defensive zone when entering the country, becoming the target for fortification activities and the concentration spot for the military units designed to defend them. The eastern border of the Bohemian crownlands with the Kingdom of Hungary was also the border between Hungary and Moravia and Hungary and Silesia. This became evident especially in the 16th century in the structure of the units designed for border protection. Warfare in the turbulent Hungarian times, the advancement of the Ottoman Army, and the continuing threat of the Hungarian anti-Habsburg uprising, which lasted throughout the 17th century, represented a permanent danger. The border with Hungary was therefore a place whose defence attracted the attention of estate representatives and later also the highest military bodies of Moravia and Silesia. The forms of military and paramilitary units represented a complex organizational structure; the defence of the country was secured by both the state (royal) and the provincial (estate) units, as well as the paramilitary units of the subjects (inhabitants) living in the border areas. This development reflected qualitative changes in the military sector, and the far-reaching consequences of the process also had a societal impact. The process can be concisely summarised within the historiographical concept of 'military revolution'. The present contribution follows the above-mentioned issues primarily through investigating the development of irregular armed forces formed of local citizens, which were deployed in border protection.

Chapter 4 - Since 2008 the Hungarian fiscal and monetary policy have been changed radically as a consequence of worldwide crisis. The new policy provided economic stability, but long-lasting cultural imbalance persisted. The renewed economic regulations managed several issues *pro futuro* but did not provide any solutions for the existing problem of debtors in Hungary. Although financial and economic reconstruction, the raising of the level of employment, the continuous cutdown of the prime interest rate, the lower interest of commercial banks and the higher GDP promoted the consolidation of the domestic loan market, they helped both individuals and enterprises, but the crash left behind a deep impact on Hungarian society. The author guesses neither the masses nor the State are getting ready for a new economic crisis, which is due to happen in the near future. The author strongly believes that a new economic crisis is going to result in sweeping changes in the Hungarian society. The study makes an attempt to prove that the financial knowledge of individuals, the level of the financial culture of a nation and mainly the convenient national/ supranational financial regulation (including the state protection of consumers) determine fundamentally the situation of future generations. The authors have to see clearly that there is a close correlation between the financial (realized or failed) policy (legislation) and the structure of future society. The object of this study - focusing mainly on the monetary policy – is to demonstrate those instruments by which an excessively polarized society could be prevented in the near future.

In: An In Depth Look at Hungary
Editor: Esperanta Rompa
ISBN: 978-1-53615-351-4

Chapter 1

HEALTH INEQUALITY AND ITS REGIONAL DISPARITIES IN HUNGARY: A CASE STUDY ON THE ROLE OF ACCESS TO HEALTH CARE

Annamaria Uzzoli[1,*]*, Attila Bán*[2]*, Szilvia Beke*[3]
and Viktor Pál[4] *and József Vitrai*[5]
[1]Institute for Regional Studies, Centre for Economic and Regional Studies, Hungarian Academy of Sciences, Budapest, Hungary
[2]Katona József Library of Bács-Kiskun County, Kecskemét, Hungary
[3]Faculty of Health and Social Science, Gál Ferenc University College, Gyula, Hungary
[4]Department of Economic and Human Geography, University of Szeged, Szeged, Hungary
[5]National Center for Public Health, Budapest, Hungary

* Corresponding Author's Email: uzzoli@rkk.hu.

ABSTRACT

There are numerous studies relating to health inequalities highlighting the role of access to health care. However this research is usually focussed on regional distribution of that care. Our case study made in Hungary is based on quantitative and qualitative examinations which describes the connection between health inequalities and barriers of accessibility. With this context in mind, this chapter aims to analyse the Hungarian health inequalities in terms of space and time, after the political and economic transition of 1989, defining the influence of accessibility on those inequalities.

Therefore this chapter contains three main structural parts, which aim to identify the theoretical background and empirical results with its primary conclusions, regarding Hungarian health inequalities and difficulties in accessing those services. Firstly, our aims and methods are clearly shown, to give an easier understanding of the scientific and empirical framework in our research. Additionally, we have strongly highlighted importantance of international and Hungarian preliminaries as very different approaches in defining the role of accessibility in health inequalities. Then, statistical analyses can help to discover how mortality rates and life expectancies have changed timely and spatially in Hungary in the last more than 25 years. The following section highlights the most informative experiences of the presented national and local case studies on examining primary barriers in access to health care. The unequal access to health care often varies according to the type of health service, which is the main reason that the case study is focusing on the area of infarction care through one of noncommunicable diseases such as acute myocardial infarction. Likewise, some local barriers and availabilities in access to infarction care are also explained. There are based on making on semi-structured interviews with health care stakeholders. Finally, some areas and mechanisms of decision-making are studied by content-analysis according to the Hungarian health policy strategies and concepts.

The major conclusion of this chapter is that socio-economic inequalities are one of the most relevant barriers in access to health care which might leading to increased health inequalities.

Keywords: health inequality, access to health care, regional differences, acute myocardial infarction, Hungary

INTRODUCTION

Barriers of access to health care services may play an important part in understanding determinative factors of health inequalities. Despite considerable public health interventions, marked differences in health exist among and within countries today. The interpretation of the socio-economic indicators defining health inequalities, presumes that not only does health status count from a health point of view, but also the level and growth of already existing health inequalities within a country and their typical spatial pattern.

Access to health care has a key role in the performance of health care systems all around the world. Health care services should be available, accessible, acceptable and of high quality from the perspectives of patients, regardless of their gender distribution or socio-economic status (The Global Health 50/50 Report, 2018). Access to health care as well as health inequality is basically a multifactorial definition and can be conceptualized in many ways. However, the term of accessibility often used to describe determinative factors and socio-economic characteristics of health inequality (Levesque et al., 2013; Waters, 2000; Whitehead, 1992). This is the main reason that access to health care remains such a complex issue within our study. This is illustrated by the varying interpretations of the concept across health inequalities.

The general state of health of the Hungarian people is worse than justified by the level of economic development (Egri and Tánczos, 2015; Józan, 1994a; Uzzoli, 2016). The deterioration in the state of health, which had been on-going since the middle of the 1960s, turned into an epidemiological crisis by the early 1990s, and impacted the entire adult population (Józan, 1994a, 1994b, 1996). From the second half of the 1990s, Hungary has faced substantial improvements in many health outcomes, but the country is still lagging behind many of the more developed countries. The majority of the main health indicators are worse than the average of OECD's values, that indicates Hungary belongs to the middle-ground of countries in the world according to the general state of health of its population. More poor health outcomes are linked together with significant regional disparities in the country and these larger and relative spatial inequalities are especially observed between Western and Eastern parts of Hungary.

The aim of this chapter is to discover regional differences in health inequalities in Hungary, with special emphasis on accessibility. On the one hand, the focus is on determining how difficulties in access to health care may has effect on health inequalities. But on the other hand, it also looks at how health inequalities and barriers of accessibility are influenced by locality. The chapter consists of three major structural parts. Firstly, the scientific background, which helps us to define the role of accessibility in health inequalities. But it also summarizes the most relevant preliminary researches to interpreting and explaining the Hungarian approach to this issue. Secondly, statistical analyses can show us how health inequalities have changed in terms of space and time after the Hungarian economic and political transition of 1989. Thirdly, a case study on empirical examination of how accessibility presents the major difficulties in access to health care, which can influence health inequality and its spatial distribution in Hungary. This case study is a part of a three year course research project, which is based on studying the connection between health inequalities and accessibility (with the example one of cardiovascular diseases such as the chronic disease of acute myocardial infarction) (NKFIA, 2016).

Methodologically, our examinations were integrated both of quantitative and qualitative techniques as mixed methods. Using mixed methods to evaluate health services is increasingly often applied in health research (Tariq and Woodmann, 2013; Wisdom and Creswell, 2013). In quantitative approaches, official statistics were used as the basis of this chapter, completed data from other sources, such as internet or institutional medical database was also used. Desk research was also used to create content-analysis and secondary data analysis. Qualitative approaches tend to generate non-numerical data, using methods such as semi-structured interviews as part of a fieldwork. Additionally, the wide range of special literature was also used as a secondary source.

Our results and experiences suggest that there is a clear link between barriers in access to health care services and inequitable distribution of a noncommunicable disease in Hungary. In the long term, it can give comprehensive information for evidence based health policy as a reducer and preventer of health inequalities.

The following section focuses on the scientific background of this chapter, particularly on some of the most common characteristics of the difficulties in access to health care according to the different international and Hungarian approaches.

SCIENTIFIC BACKGROUND

Defining the concept of access to health care as well as health inequality is not an easy task, because there are a number of different approaches and definitions. What is more, the definition can often depend on the performance of conceptualisation, because it can be conceptualized in numerous ways. It is generally defined as access to a health service, a health provider or a health institution, thus defined as the opportunity with which consumers or communities are able to use appropriate services in proportion to their needs (Daniels, 1982; Whitehead, 1992). However, the complex notion of access to health care is based on varying interpretations of different concept across approaches and authors. Here are some of them:

- The term access to health care is often used to define determinative factors and socio-economic characteristics influencing health inequality (e.g., Braveman, 2003).
- Many approaches put more emphasis on the characteristics of health care resources (e.g., Donabedian, 1990).
- Some approaches highlight that access to health care describes the adjustment between the individual and the health care system, because it intermediates the relationship between demand and supply of health services (e.g., Penchansky and Thomas, 1981).
- Some authors use behavioral model to provide measures of access to medical/health care, and in this approach potential access is

simply defined as the presence of enabling resources which can realize equitable and inequitable access (e.g., Andersen, 1995).

- It is important suggestion for policy-makers that ensuring equity in acces is not just about increasing service provision, because an one-sizefits-all approach to access to health care can lead to discrimination against those whose needs remain unrecognized (e.g., Napier et al., 2017).
- Equity of access may be measured in terms of '5A' dimensions of health care access as approachability, acceptability, availability, affordability, appropriateness (e.g., Gulliford et al., 2002).
- Most studies have observed an unequal access to health care or an unequal use of health services is generated by existing socio-economic inequalities as well as health inequalities (Almeida et al., 2017; Levesque et al., 2013). The unequal access to health care is usually varying according to the type of service used.

Searching the evidence in 'Web of Science Core Collection' can confirm increasing relevance of studying the role of access to health care in health inequalities. Web of Science is an unified research platform that can help find more indepth information about a wide variety of content (Web of Science, 2018). In this case, we could analyse publications and citations between 1975 and 2017 based on term of access to health care (Figure 1).

From the middle of the 1970s the first publications appeared focusing on access to health care and barriers were presented (e.g., Donabedian, 1973), but until the beginning of the 1990s the number of these publications with their citation was quite low. A continuous and notable increasing tendency seems from the beginning of the 2000s, which could result marked importance for this scientific topic in number of publications as well as in citations. Examining access to health care and its difficulties is an area of current research both nationally and internationally. Additionally, analysing health consequences and outcomes related to the latest economic crisis of 2008/2012 also contributed to highlight this issue.

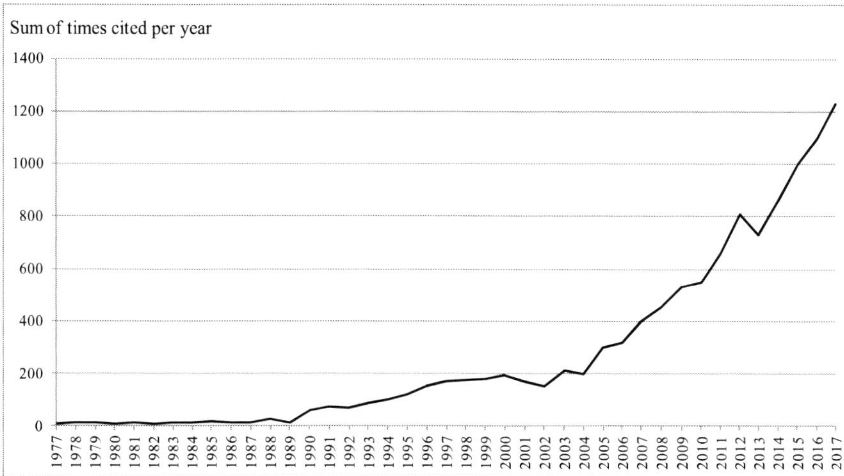

Data source: Web of Science Core Collection.

Figure 1. Citation report with the title of 'access to health care' from Web of Science Core Collection, 1977-2017.

The investigation of the role and importance of the access to health care is also a common research theme in the Hungarian literature. Due to its interdisciplinary nature, also representatives of different disciplines studied the evolution of the role of health inequality. However, in contrast to the approach taken in the international investigations of access, it often appears indirectly: the Hungarian authors usually studying health inequality and get a number of results, which carry information on inequity in access of care. This is the reason that most of these publications do not mention access, but they study precisely its inequality directly or indirectly. Summarizing the most important Hungarian studies in this field it can be concluded that, in essence, they all apply three different dominant research concepts:

1. A number of researchers found the inequality of access to health care can be originated in a lack of resources of health care. Mainly in studies on primary health care, it stated that the main cause of inequality of access to health care might be the deficit in human resources. (Kovács et al., 2013; Orosz and Kollányi 2016). The relationship between the availability of resources and the

accessibility of care arose in particular in the investigations of the 2008-2012 economic crisis health consequences. Some authors have found that recession could increase the need of care, coupled with a reduced expenditure on health – as an obstacle to access – simply creating more social inequalities (Orosz, 2013). Others have drawn attention to the fact that in times of crisis the healthy lifestyle options are commonly reduced, for example, as a result of unemployment and declining incomes (Uzzoli, 2011).

2. A growing number of research groups interpret that access inequality exists through the physical barriers, such as distance, poor road conditions as poor availability of transportation, and peripheral geographical location (Kemkers et al., 2010; Kiss, 2013; Kiss and Mattányi, 2005). With this standpoint the question of geographical location is highlighted, especially through settlement hierarchy and spatial considerations. Several authors also conclude that the geographical locations of health institutions and health service availability depend on the size of the settlements, and population figures, also the its socio-economic development of a particular area (Egri, 2016; Kiss, 2016).
3. Part of the behavioral model, partly through the adoption of inequality model more Hungarian authors have come to the conclusion, that an individual level, or lack of financial resources, or the low level of health literacy at macroeconomic level and the socio-economic development could be the main factors impeding access to health care (e.g., Kovács and Tóth, 2015; Kovai, 2017; Pál, 2017; Vitrai et al., 2008 etc.).

It seems evident that the previous Hungarian studies, as with several international investigations, applied a multidisciplinary approach and studied the opportunities and barriers of the access to health care. It can be concluded that the explicit or implicit role of the access to care might be the explanatory factor mainly in formatting and sustaining of health inequality.

A brief synthesis of the published and the most cited specific international and domestic literature (on the definition and the conceptualization of access to health care) served to help us create a conceptual framework for our research. In addition, we also accessed the most important authoritative Hungarian preliminaries to identify the characteristics of access to health care, using them in our research. Firstly, we looked at access to health care as the opportunity to present health care needs with using health care services and looked to identify any gap between them. It is also useful to examine how patients can reach and access health services. Secondly, our investigations lead us to conclude that the access to and the use of health care are not synonymous in our research. The use of health services denotes direct contact with health services has been made and it provides us the evidence that access has therefore been achieved. Thirdly, we are able to conclude barriers in the access to and the use of health care are an expression of the characteristics of health inequalities. Finally, we accept that socio-economic characteris-tics can influence the spatial patterns of access to health care.

The following section focuses on statistical analysis of this chapter, and mainly on some of the features of the Hungarian health inequality with its spatial pattern regarding access to health care.

Changes of the Hungarian Health Inequality in Terms of Space and Time after 1989

Health inequalities can be defined as differences in health status or in the distribution of health determinants between different population groups and social classes. Moreover, health inequalities not only imply social or spatial inequalities, but also socio-spatial inequalities as a whole (Jones and Moon, 1987). It is also important to recognize that health inequalities have spatial aspects that reflect the social context of health inequalities. This is main reason that we decided to apply the approach of health inequalities to present how the most important health indicators have changed in terms of space and time after 1989.

The collapse of the communist system in Hungary 1989 resulted new political, economic and social situation. These essential changes also took place in the Eastern European countries from the end of the 1980s and from the beginning of the 1990s. The transformation in these former socialist countries also have had gone together with demographic and health challenges. The turn of the 1980/1990s years with the change of regime became one of the most important periods in the history of Hungary. Consequences of this transition in health and health care have led to deterioration of health in the population. Poor Hungarian health conditions were not unique among the European post-socialist countries, because all of them faced similar unfavourable health processes at that time. The social effects of the transformation such as the acute problems of unemployment and poverty among low-income population groups have caused 'health recession' and decreasing tendency in life expectancy. So called 'East Central European health paradox' was a typical health situation in the post-socialist countries (Egri-Tánczos, 2015). It means that there was a strikingly high rate of premature mortality in these transforming societies, while the epidemiological crisis has associated with a decreasing tendency in life expectancy across all age groups of adult population (Cornia and Paniccia, 2000; Skrabski et al., 2003, 2004). This European region, including Hungary, has showed a worse morbidity and mortality situation than was justified based on the economic situation in the early of the 1990s (Egri and Tánczos, 2015; Józan, 1994a; Uzzoli, 2016).

Nevertheless the marked deterioration in the state of health of the Hungarian population did not begin in the 1990s, it had been on the increase since the middle of the 1960s (Józan, 1994a, 1994b). As a consequence of this trend, Hungary is presently lagging behind the post-socialist countries, as well as the more developed countries according to the main health indicators. The decades-long worsening of health indicators with poor health conditions have resulted an internationally disadvantaged position for Hungary. Knowledge of a country's average life expectancy at birth, is a good indicator in understanding the international position of a country according to health culture as well as the general standard of health of the population.

A country's life expectancy is most commonly linked with indicators that measure the social, economic, and environmental well-being of the country and its citizens. For example, generally people living in countries with higher GNI per capita, tend to have longer life expectancies and lower infant mortality rates etc. 72.0 years was the average life expectancy at birth of the global population in 2016. Hungary's life expectancy was higher than the global average with its 75.8 years in 2016 (79.2 years for female, 72.4 years for male). Hungary is belonging to the upper-middle-life expectancy group in the world, because countries with the highest life expectancy are recorded at over over 80.0 years, middle-life expectancy of this group is between 70.0 and 79.9 years.

Available data for 183 countries of WHO shows that Hungary has a relatively high premature mortality rate among other member countries. Generally Hungary's international position is relative to other countries of the world, but it appears worse than the average of the most developed Western European countries, based on premature mortality. This relative position also presents a paradox situation at the same time: on the one hand, premature death due to noncommunicable diseases appears to have improved, but on the other hand, a deterioration in the ranking position has occurred between 2000 and 2016 (Table 1). During this period the rate of premature death has decreased, while the ranking position has deteriorated a little, based on descending order of premature mortality values of the countries. The lack of long-term improvement in premature death due to noncommunicable diseases is particularly pronounced among the Hungarian male population.

Noncommunicable diseases (NCDs), such as heart disease, stroke, cancer, chronic respiratory diseases, chronic digestive diseases or diabetes, are the leading cause of mortality in the developed countries of world. NCDs are estimated to account for 93% of all deaths in Hungary (Figure 2). Main causes of death and its distribution is similar to other developed countries and meets the model of health (epidemiological) transition (Gaál et al., 2011; Omran, 2005). Cardiovascular diseases and cancers are the leading death causes, but their rates are higher than the average of all members of the European Union (EU-28). Especially, cardiovascular death rates show a significant gap between Hungary and EU-28 countries. These are influenced by many collective and individual factors such as socio-economic situation, quality of health care system, health behaviour etc. There is a wide variety of health promotion and prevention measures for national health systems which can bring about changes to reduce health risks of noncommunicable diseases related to premature deaths. Although, barriers in access to health care can reduce the efficiency of the measures in health promotion and prevention.

Table 1. Hungary's important health indicator as premature mortality from WHO Health Statistics 2000, 2016

Health indicator	**2000**		**2016**	
	Value (%)	Ranking position*	Value (%)	Ranking position*
Noncommunicable disease (NCD) deaths under age 70 (percent of all NCD deaths) in Hungary (%), both genders	39%	45.	33%	46.
Noncommunicable disease (NCD) deaths under age 70 (percent of all NCD deaths) in Hungary (%), female	28%	42.	23%	43.
Noncommunicable disease (NCD) deaths under age 70 (percent of all NCD deaths) in Hungary (%), male	50%	56.	44%	59.

Data source: www.who.int.

Legend: * Ranking position of Hungary among the members of World Health Organization (WHO) based on descending order of premature mortality values of the countries.

The interpretation of health inequalities commonly depend on a country's macroeconomic conditions, which are always linked to socio-economic inequalities regarding the unfairness of the distribution system. In addition bad labour market position, difficulties in the availability of health care and education, disadvantaged living and life conditions and little chance of a healthy life are also contributing factors. Defining health inequalities from a health point of view, presumes the use of average life expectancy at birth statistics, because this index reflects the overall mortality level of a population (Johnston et al., 2000). Life expectancy also depends on the improvement or the worsening of the mortality situation and summarizes the mortality patterns that prevails across all age groups (Wilkinson, 1996). This is the main reason to analyse the indicators of mortality rate and average life expectancy at birth, because both of them related to health inequalities and their changes in terms of space and time.

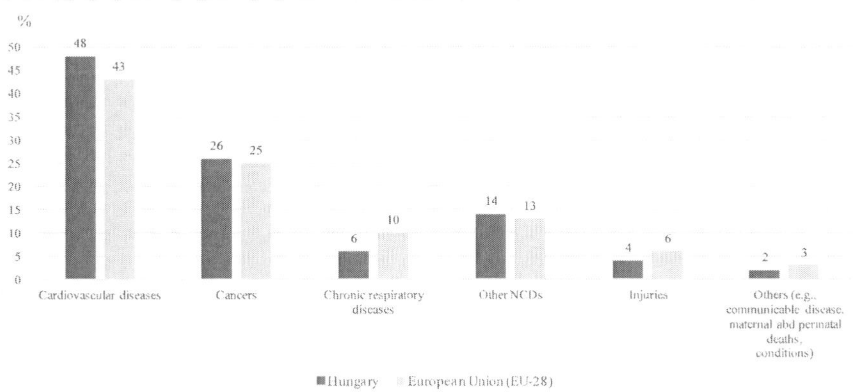

Data source: Statistical Yearbooks of Hungary.

Figure 2. Proportional mortality in Hungary and in the European Union, 2016.

The deep economic crisis around the time of the regime change had a significant impact on the Hungarian health processes within a very short period of time. Coincidentally, the worsening trend in mortality rate in Hungary after the transition in 1989 showed a similar pattern to most other Central and Eastern European countries. (Uzzoli, 2016) (Figure 3). As in all of the former communist states after the political and economic transformation, a growing trend in higher mortality rate was evidenced, which led to a period of deterioration in health status through the decrease in life expectancy (Figure 4). This unfavourable tendency was caused by the increase in the number and rate of premature mortality from the beginning of the 1990s as the dramatic consequence of the transformation on the middle-aged population (e.g., due to unemployment, financial uncertainty, decreased social safety). This was followed by new, unprecedented worsening of life expectancies in Hungary.

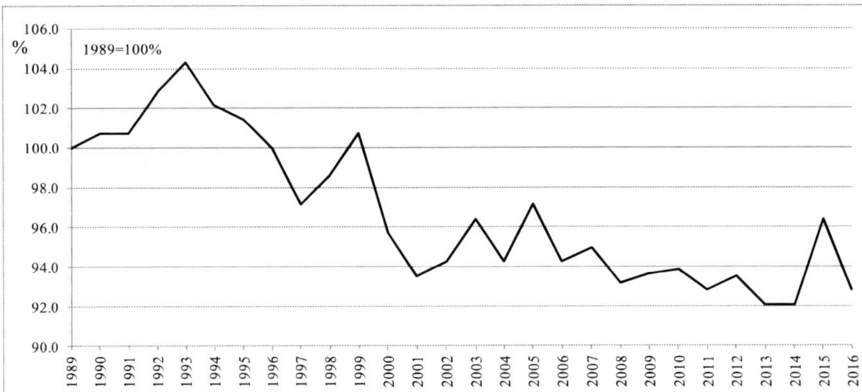

Data source: Statistical Yearbooks of Hungary.

Figure 3. Mortality rate in the proportion of 1989 in Hungary between 1989 and 2016.

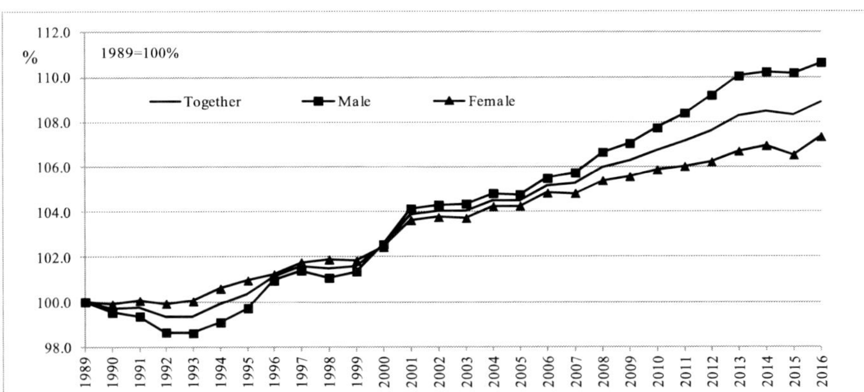

Data source: Statistical Yearbooks of Hungary.

Figure 4. Average life expectancy at birth by gender in the proportion of 1989 in Hungary between 1989 and 2016 (1989 = 100%).

The epidemiological crisis has reached its bottom in 1993 with the worst rate of mortality and the lowest point of life expectancy, which was particularly prevalent among men. After this period of epidemiological crisis, slow and moderate improvement of life expectancy began from 1995.

The gradual rise in life expectancy was more emphasised among men. Female life expectancy stagnated from the period of the latest economic crisis, with the result of increasing gap between male and female life expectancy. Moreover, men's life expectancy also stagnated in the latest years. The difference between male and female life expectancy has increased since 1989, and this was reflected to the reduction in Hungary's relative international position.

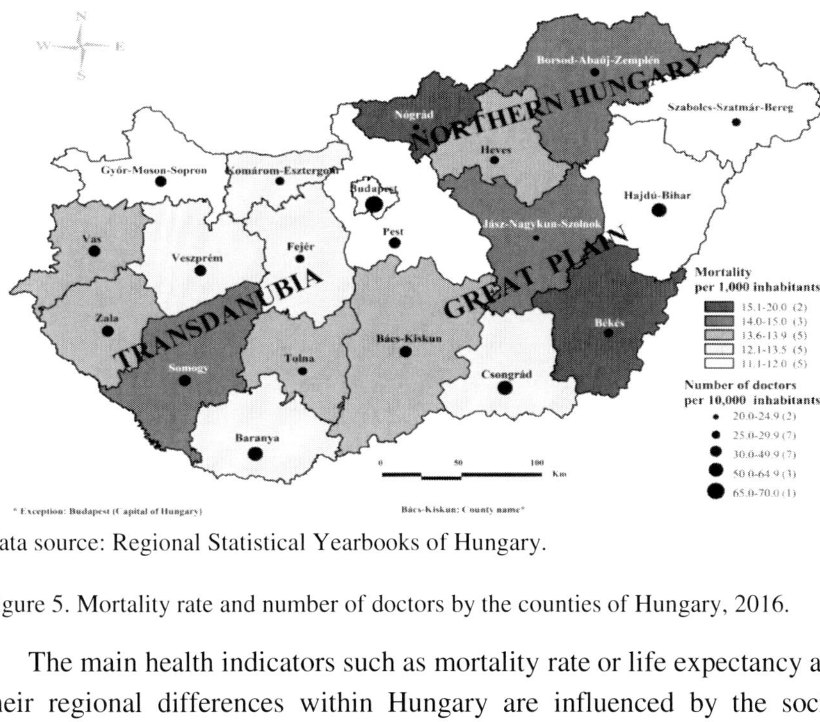

Data source: Regional Statistical Yearbooks of Hungary.

Figure 5. Mortality rate and number of doctors by the counties of Hungary, 2016.

The main health indicators such as mortality rate or life expectancy and their regional differences within Hungary are influenced by the socio-economic inequalities. These inequalities can influence the patterns of use of health services and can also exert an important influence on the access to health care. For instance, in addition to the strong association with income, individuals with better socio-economic situation tend to have greater ease in recognizing a health need and ability to seek the required care service.

Considerable divergences are shown between the different parts of the country according to mortality rate and number of doctors (Figure 5). The spatial gap is well-marked between Western and Eastern parts of the country. Budapest as the capital and its surrounding area showing the best figures. Moreover, 'a spatial axis' is drawn up along the line of four counties as Nógrád, Heves, Jász-Nagykun-Szolnok and Békés. This axis functions as a dividing line in Hungary and divides it clearly into Western and Eastern parts of the country. The most favourable counties based on lower level of mortality with higher number of doctors are in the North Western part of Hungary including the capital, while the most unfavourable areas can be found in the South Western and North Eastern parts of the country. In this latter case, Szabolcs-Szatmár-Bereg County shows a paradox situation. The main health indicators remained below the national level after 1989, but currently there is a remarkable improvement in mortality rates which could probably result a relative better health position for Hungary in the future. To evaluate regional inequalities within a county it is more useful to apply micro-regional level in statistical analyses, because it can give more sophisticated information about spatial pattern and the locality of health processes.

Micro-level data on average life expectancy at birth by gender and its changes in terms of space and time can also help to confirm health inequalities present in Hungary (Figure 6, Figure 7). Between 1991 and 2016 important changes have occurred within the country and these changes can strengthen the Western-Eastern division in Hungary. Firstly, there are not any districts at micro-regional level in Hungary, where life expectancy would have been worse in 2016 than in 1991. It means life expectancy has increased in both of genders continuously across all districts, especially from the second half of the 1990s (see Figure 4). Secondly, a spectacular increase in life expectancy has touched those areas of the country where life expectancies were originally among the worst since 1989 (e.g., Southern Transdanubia, Northern Hungary, Northern Great Plain). The relative positions of the different regions in relation to each other have not changed or have hardly changed in the past more than 25 years. "*The most advantaged and worst disadvantaged regions or areas were the same at the beginning of the 1990s as today*" (Uzzoli, 2016. p. 154.). Thirdly, more significant improvement has occurred among Hungarian males and this is the consequence of the epidemiological crisis, because it had affected more men rather than women with its more remarkable differences in health status. Fourthly, the spatial pattern of life expectancies based on its changes between 1991 and 2016 is quite mosaic according to female's life expectancy.

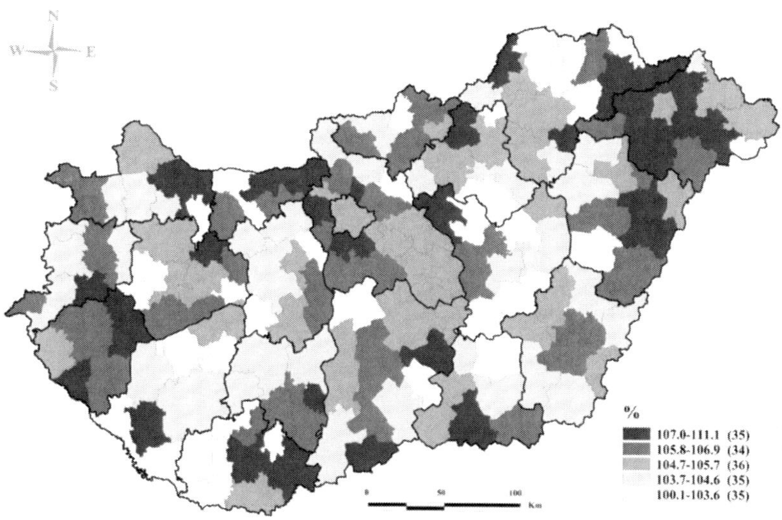

Data source: Regional Statistical Yearbooks of Hungary.

[Note: After 1989 health indicators were published firstly at micro-regional level in Hungary in 1991.]

Figure 6. Female average life expectancy at birth in the proportion of 1991 at micro-regional level in Hungary, 2016 (1991 = 100%).

More homogenious spatial patterns of changing life expectancy among men refers to long-term health effects of epidemiological crisis because it has targeted mainly middle-aged men n living in economically declining regions after the transition of 1989 (e.g., in Szabolcs-Szatmár-Bereg County). Whereas the lowest level of increasing life expectancy by both of genders confirms the duality or dichotomy of the country, because many of the districts with the lowest levels are located in the Eastern part of Hungary.

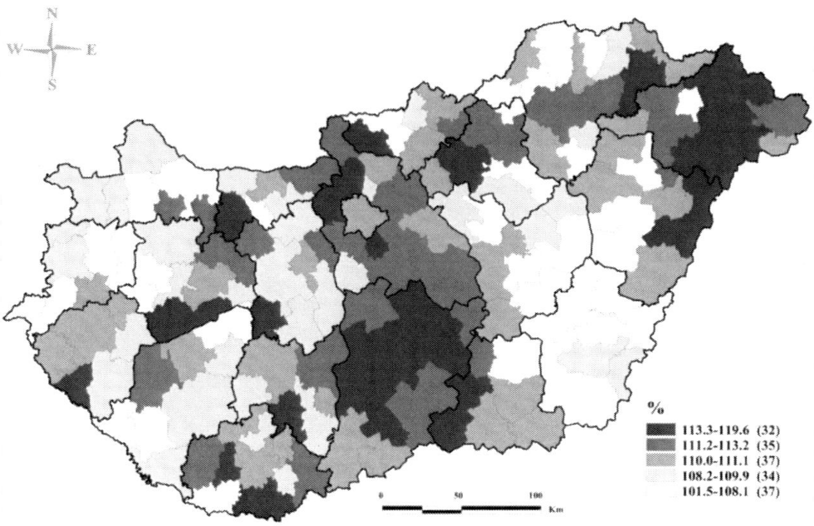

Data source: Regional Statistical Yearbooks of Hungary.

[Note: After 1989 health indicators were published at micro-regional level in Hungary firstly in 1991.]

Figure 7. Male average life expectancy at birth in the proportion of 1991 at micro-regional level in Hungary, 2016 (1991 = 100%).

Improving life expectancy went together with increasing regional inequalities in Hungary in the past more than 25 years (Table 2). After the transition in 1989 a deterioration in mortality has resulted decreasing life expectancy, nevertheless from the middle of the 1990s continuous but slow increasing tendency is a current health process. Beside this favourable trend, regional inequalities of life expectancy have started to grow and now there are significant differences between different parts of the country. The differentiation is more remarkable among women rather than among men. All of districts with the worst values of life expectanncy can be found in the Eastern part of the country while the best values are belonging to the Western part of Hungary.

Table 2. Regional inequalities of average life expectancy at birth by gender in Hungary (years), 1991, 2016

Health indicator	Minimum value (years)	District of minimum value and its geographical location	Maximum value (years)	District of maximum value and its geographical location	Difference between minimum and maximum value (years)
Average life expectancy at birth, female, 1991	69.8	Tokaji (Northern Hungary)	77.0	Balatonalmádi (Transdanubia)	7.2
Average life expectancy at birth, male, 1991	57.6	Tokaji (Northern Hungary)	67.4	Siófoki (Transdanubia)	9.8
Average life expectancy at birth, female, 2016	72.9	Bélapátfalvai (Northern Hungary)	81.9	Vasvári (Transdanubia)	9.0
Average life expectancy at birth, male, 2016	65.9	Ózdi (Northern Hungary)	76.0	Balatonfüredi (Transdanubia)	10.1

Data source: www.ksh.hu.

It is clear that after 1989 the worsening of mortality indicators such as life expectancy were part of a decade-long worsening of the health process. Clearly, this decade-long worsening health process has resulted an epidemiological crisis in Hungary up to 1993. Afterwards, this worsening tendency stopped from the middle of the 1990s. The mortality rate has stabilized, albeit at a high level. As a result life expectancy has increased slowly, but it has led to the epidemiological change in Hungary. Hungary's internationally poor position among the more developed countries represents as one of the worst in Central and Eastern Europe. The improvements in life expectancy were out of step with the economic performance and growth within Hungary, significant regional disparities within the country remain apparent (Uzzoli, 2016). The socio-economic division of Hungary demonstrates the dichotomy of health inequalities, and the widening health gap between the Eastern and Western halves of the country.

In light of results based on statistical analyses when examining changes related to Hungarian health inequalities (in terms of space and time) refer in a complex way to the barriers of access to health care such as disadvantageous labour market situation, lower income levels, unfavourable living conditions, worse level of health behaviour. In our research project the main aim is to describe health inequalities present in Hungary today. The other aim is to show how different barriers in access to health care can influence regional disparities of morbidity and mortality. Our case study highlights the area of cardivascular diseases (such as acute myocardial infarction, AMI) which is an appropriate medical condition in many ways for studying regional and local factors in relation to access to health care.

The following section of this chapter focuses on presenting the most important results and experiences of our quantitative and qualitative examinations to explore primary barriers and possibilities in access to infarction care in Hungary.

Examining Barriers in Access to Health Care: A Case Study on Acute Myocardial Infarction and Its Inequality at National and Local Level in Hungary

Interpreting the role of access to the Hungarian health care system and proving its regional inequality are shwon here via features of care related to acute myocardial infarction (AMI). The disease is a good indicator of the possible difficulties and barriers of the access to health care. On the one hand, it increases the chance of survival in short term if the patient gets PCI (percutaneous coronary intervention) right after the first symptoms of infarction. On the other hand, in long term it increases the recovery and the chance of survival over 30 days if the patient gets rehabilitation care right after the acute treatment (Belicza et al., 2016; Hagen et al., 2015). (It is the reason why we have used the treatment of infarction in order to find supporting and barrier factors of access to health care in the case study of the research.)

Statistical data analyses have confirmed that after the changing of the political system in 1989 we have seen worsening, improving and stagnating tendencies in connection with cardiovascular mortality (Figure 8). Increasing rates are tied to crises situations such as the epidemiological crisis in 1993 or the most recent economic crisis of 2008/2009.

Data source: Health Statistical Yearbooks of Hungary.

Figure 8. Cardiovascular mortality rate in the proportion of 1989 in Hungary between 1989 and 2015 (1989 = 100%).

It is a fact that since the middle of the 2000s the mortality rate of circulatory system improved, however over the past few years there has been a increase in data. The main cause of the decrease related to circulatory system mortality is the reduction in the proportion of ischemic heart diseases during the past 15 years (Figure 9). However, health effects of the most recent economic crisis moderately increased in mortality rates caused by ischemic heart diseases in Hungary. Since the middle of the 2000s the mortality rate of AMI examined in detail among ischemic heart diseases also has a decreasing tendency (Figure 10). Since then the mortality rate has halved which can be experienced mainly among men. Nowadays nearly twice the number of men who die in infarction than women in Hungary though. Although in the past few years this trend has shifted back to effect of increase in the female infarction mortality rate as well. The noticeable improvement of infarction mortality during the past 15 years is attributed to the increasing number of PCI centres and the expansion of their capacity.

The previous statistical data analysis has confirmed that:

- the incidence of AMI is higher in all age groups in case of males rather than in case of females,
- males in all age groups can access to percutaneous coronary intervention (PCI) with better outcomes,
- generally in cases of fatality, the early death occurs within 30 days after infarction (Belicza and Jánosi, 2012).

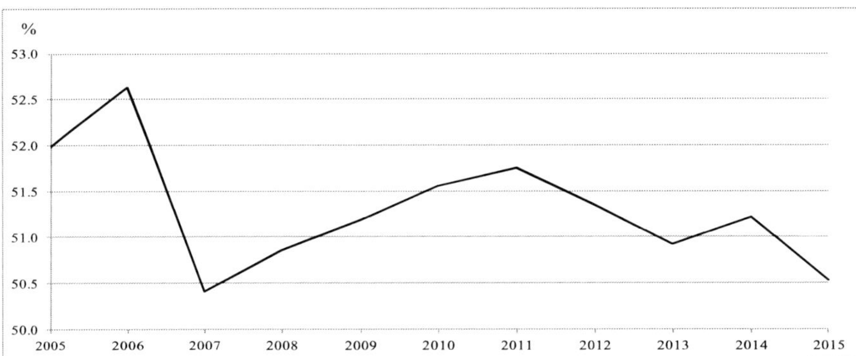

Data source: Health Statistical Yearbooks of Hungary.
[Note: Data for ischemic heart diseases are only available from 2005.]

Figure 9. Rate of ischemic heart diseases in the proportion of total cardiovascular mortality (standardized death rate per 100,000) in Hungary between 2005 and 2015.

In Hungary the improvement in data related to infarction mortality creates a paradox situation. The continuously reducing mortality rate has not affected both genders equally and in the past few years there has been a worsening in the female infarction rate. Besides the improvement is accompanied by an increase of regional differences which also affected mainly women (Figure 11, Figure 12). There are more and more regional differences throughout the country, moreover in some certain regions the mortality rate of infarction increased up to 2015 compared to 2005.

Consequently the improvement, namely the decrease inmortality has not affected the districts equally at micro-regional level. The increasing tendency can be far seen in distance from PCI centres, particularly in border and peripheral areas of the country. There are some districts in Hungary where there were 2 or 3 times more infarction mortality rate in 2015 than in 2005.

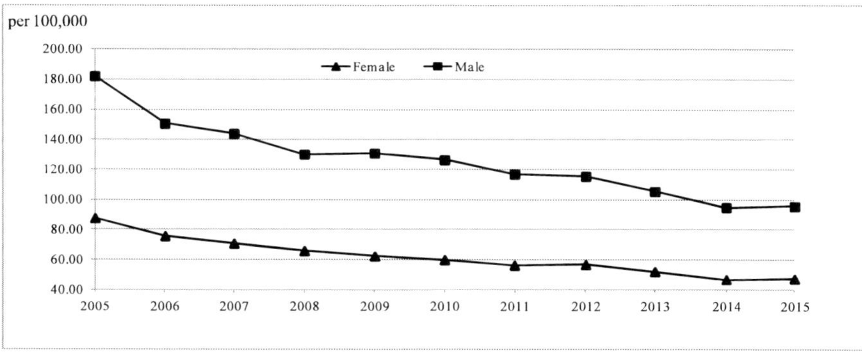

Data source: Institute for National Health Promotion.
[Note: Data for acute myocardial infarction are only available from 2005.]

Figure 10. Mortality of acute myocardial infarction (standardized death rate per 100,000 by gender) in Hungary between 2005 and 2015.

There is also a contradiction situation in AMI morbidity similarly the mortality case. The research of AMI morbidity is based on the statistical data of hospital care. There are less deaths caused by infarction due to the comprehensive introduction of PCI care, but the number of this noncommunicable disease has not improved significantly. Furthermore, there was an increasing tendency in regional differences in the middle of the 2010s compared to the middle of the 2000s.

In Hungary there are some areas where less AMI patients had access to PCI care in the period of 2012-2015 compared to the period of 2005-2008 (Figure 13). Moreover, in these areas (e.g., Fejér County, Borsod-Abaúj-Zemplén County) there are a growing number of districts at micro-regional level where AMI mortality rate has increased in the recent years.

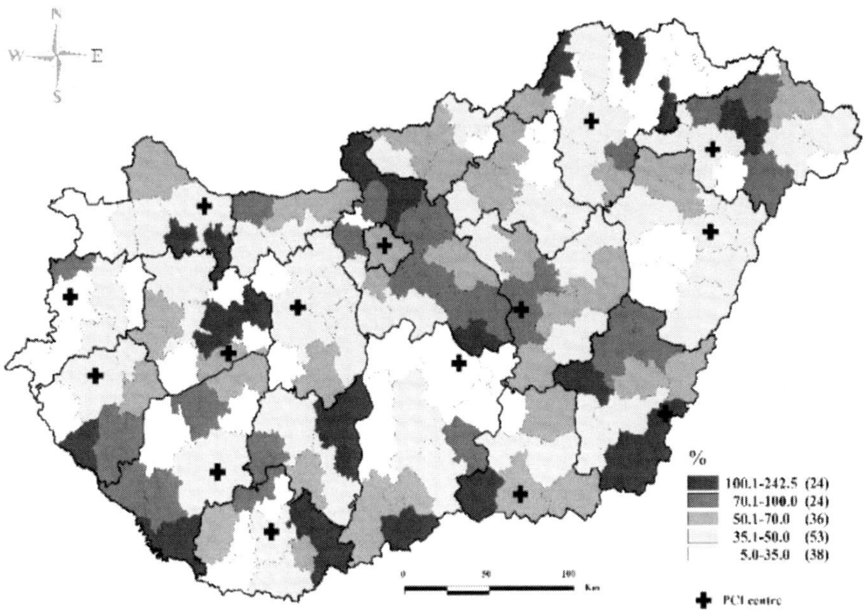

Data source: Institute for National Health Promotion.

Figure 11. Regional differences in female mortality of acute myocardial infarction (standardized death rate per 100,000) in the proportion of 2005 at micro-regional level in Hungary, 2015 (2005 = 100%).

In Hungary the paradox situation featuring infarction morbidity and mortality has resulted the moderate increase in health inequalities. According to our theoretical aspect we conclude that the increase in health inequalities can be traced back to the difficulties in access to appropriate health care. The barriers in access to health care are mainly present due to the different phases of infarction care. To analyse and confirm this we have prepared a local case study.

Statistical analysis of the research at a national level has paid attention to the different types and multileveled spatial relations of the professional and regional features of infarction care. Based on all experiences of statistical analysis the example area of the locally prepared case study was Békés County. The main viewpoints and reasons in selecting Békés County as an example area of the planned local case study were the following:

1. The health care system in Békés County is in a paradox situation for several reasons. The infrastructural improvements of health care or the slow improvement of health status refer to the favourable local health processes. Even so, the main health indicators are behind the national average.
2. The health care system of Békés County and its levels of (e.g., primary health care, out-patient care, hospital care) face significant challenges because of the nationally unfavourable morbidity and mortality situation of the local population. There are difficulties in access to local health care services based on the worst availability in some areas of the county (Beke, 2017).
3. The health conditions of the county's population are one of the most unfavourables in Hungary. Despite this fact that there have been some positive local health processes (e.g., decrease in total mortality, increase in life expectancy, improvement in health care etc.) since the middle of the 2000s.
4. Nationally unfavourable health indicators of the county are accompanied by other significant regional differences within the county which can be observed in the morbidity and mortality statistics in both genders.
5. The spatial appearance of economically and socially disadvantaged groups (e.g., ethnic minorities) contributes to the existing regional differences within the county.
6. The geographical positions of certain peripheral areas (e.g., border areas) and the generally unfavourable conditions of availability within the county (e.g., long distances, poor road conditions) significantly affect the access to the local health care.
7. The institutional background of infarction care has improved in Békés County in the past years. It could only result relative decrease in mortality while it has less effect on the number of AMI morbidity.

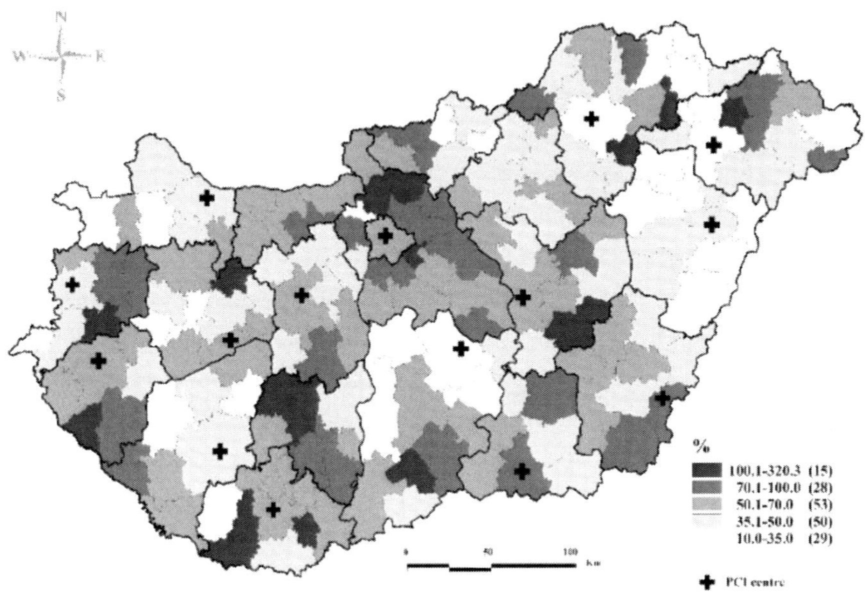

Data source: National Healthcare Services Center.

Figure 12. Regional differences in male mortality of acute myocardial infarction (standardized death rate per 100,000) in the proportion of 2005 at micro-regional level in Hungary, 2015 (2005 = 100%).

In the first phase of our local case study, desk research and its results (e.g., document analysis, regional statistical analysis) could help us to prepare interviews in the second phase of the case study. All results of the desk research have proved that since 2013 infarction mortality rate significantly decreased in Békés County due to the opening of new PCI centre in Gyula. Despite this favourable change AMI morbidity and mortality rates are high on the nation scale. It is especially true for AMI standardized death rates per 100,000 people which were higher than the national average by at least 10-30% in the case of both genders between 2005 and 2015 (Uzzoli and Beke, 2018).

The highest infarction mortality rates can be observed in the Northern (Békés and Sarkad districts at micro-regional level) and Southern part of the county (Mezőkovácsháza district) (Tóth at al., 2018). So, there are important regional differences within this county. This is based on worsening infarction morbidity situation which affects primarily women and mostly 60 years of age and under (Figure 14, Figure 15). There have been more AMI cases in the Northern and Southern part of the county effecting both genders in the period of 2012-2015 compared to the period of 2005-2008 (Figure 16, Figure 17).

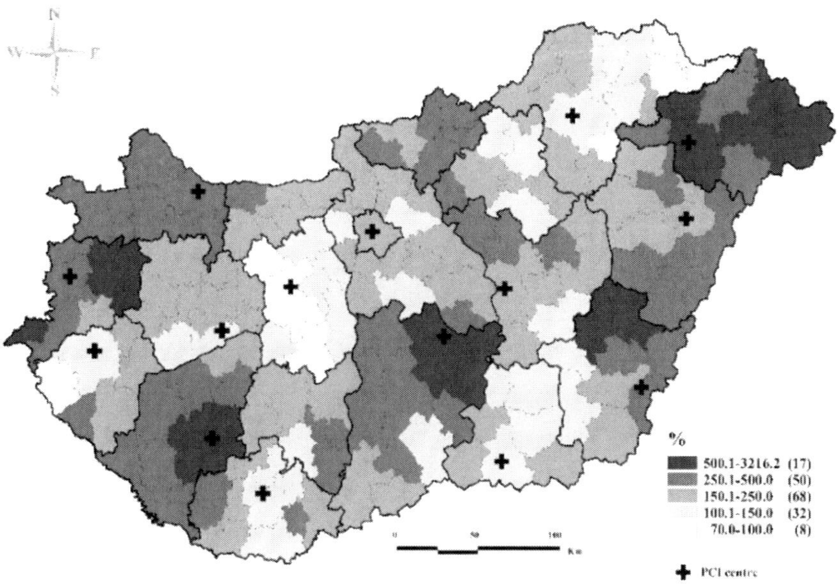

Data source: National Healthcare Services Center.

[Note: at the micro-regional level it was used a comparison of periods and not years according to the small number of acute myocardial infarction disease.]

Figure 13. Rate of patients with acute myocardial infarction who are provided percutaneous coronary interventions (PCI care) in the proportion of the period of 2005-2008 at micro-regional level of Hungary in the period of 2012-2015 (2005-2008 = 100%).

The health care system in Békés County is struggling with some specific difficulties (e.g., insufficient health promotion, less GPs etc.) nevertheless, its quality and effectiveness is not significantly behind the national average. The improvement of the morbidity situation within the county is a high priority which can be resolved with better intersectoral cooperation.

In the regional development documentation of Békés County (Integrated Regional Plan of Békés County 2014-2020, 2015) the infrastructural development plan of its primary health care sets out plans to reduce health inequality experienced at settlement level (local level). It is also important to strengthen and broaden the role of health care in the county seat of Békéscsaba by funding new health care services and the expanding of the capacity of the current services. Besides this priority it is also important to improve other treatment facilities in the hospital at Gyula. We also paid special attention to the county's demographical challenges (decreasing and ageing population).

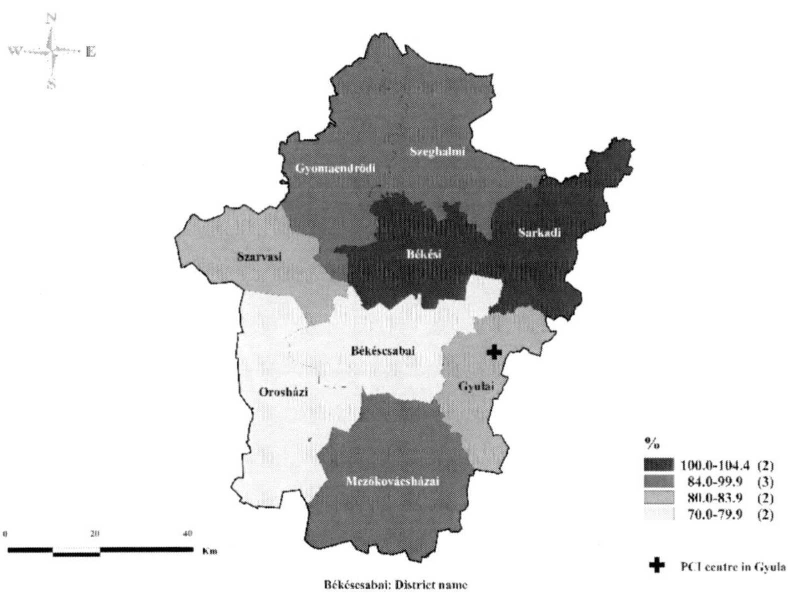

Data source: National Healthcare Services Center.

Figure 14. Morbidity rate of acute myocardial infarction among people below 60 years in the proportion of 2005-2008 at micro-regional of Békés County, Hungary, 2012-2015.

In the second phase of the planned local case study was a two-stepped part and semi-structured interviews with local medical users and stakeholders (patients and medical workers) were prepared between April and June of 2018. All the questions asked in this survey were evaluated by medical experts, and all necessary institutional permissions were obtained.

Our priority was to examine individual and institutional factors related to access to health care according to the general conditions of infarction care in Békés County. We fully investigated determinative, influencing, individual (e.g., health behaviour) and institutional (e.g., supply standards) factors which have effects on difficulties in access to health care.

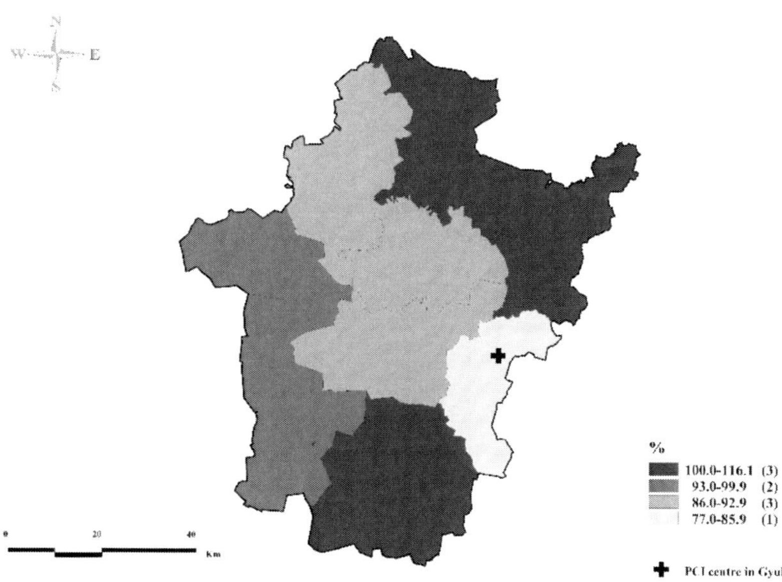

Data source: National Healthcare Services Center.

Figure 15. Female morbidity rate of acute myocardial infarction in the proportion of all infarction morbidity and in the proportion of 2005-2008 at micro-regional level of Békés County, Hungary, 2012-2015.

Firstly, altogether 24 semi-structured interviews were prepared with relevant health care providers in infarction care such as cardiologist, internist, ambulance doctor, nurse, dietetist, psychologist, physiotherapist etc. These interviews aimed to discover the professional features of organizing infarction care at county level and its general conditions and operating mechanisms. Secondly, altogether 29 semi-structured interviews were prepared with patients who had at least once acute myocardial infarction in his/her lifetime. The questions in this group of planned semi-structured interviews were addressed to define individual difficulties in access to health care. All the questions and responses are suitably paired according to the phases of infarction care such as:

- pre-hospital care: it depends on patient's hesitation (personal emergency contact times) and ambulance response times,
- hospitalization care: it is based on emergency care, cardiac catheterization, rehabilitation,
- post-hospital care: it means continuous medical controll by cardiologist and general practitioner.

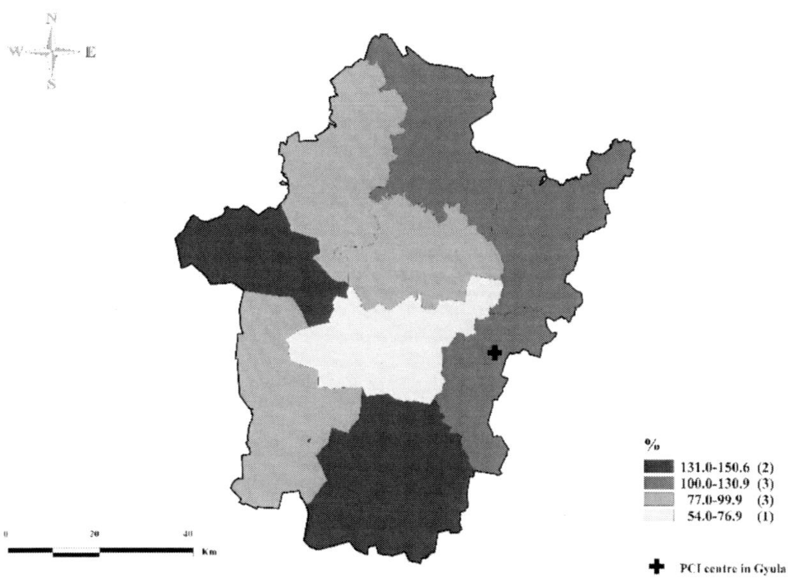

Data source: National Healthcare Services Center.

Figure 16. Female morbidity rate of acute myocardial infarction in the proportion of the county average at micro-regional level of Békés County, Hungary, 2015.

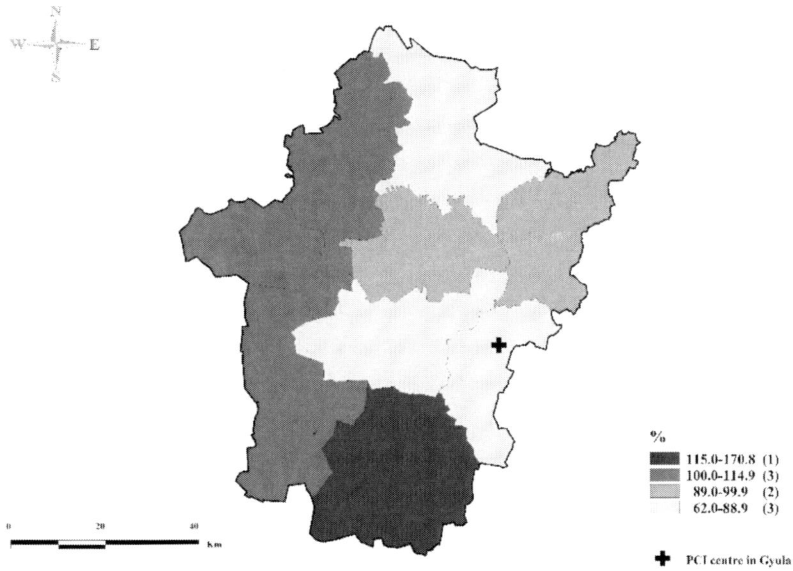

Data source: National Healthcare Services Center.

Figure 17. Male morbidity rate cute myocardial infarction in the proportion of the county average at micro-regional level of Békés County, Hungary, 2015.

After transcriptions were made, the semi-structured interviews and answers were summarized and separated into two groups. These selected two groups were based on different opinions of medical stakeholders and patients. One group was to discover those influencing factors which support access to health care. The other group of answers was to explain those influencing factors which were barriers in access to health care (Table 3, Table 4).

The semi-structured interviews prepared with local medical participants (professionals and patients) drew attention not only to the favourable changes in infarction care of Békés County in the latest years but presently existing partly operational dyfunctions as well. The support and barrier factors in access to health care are different according to the health care levels. On the other hand, these can also differ due to the health care participants' and patients' opinion (Table 3, Table 4).

Table 3. The most important influencing factors in access to health care based on semi-structured interviews made with medical stakeholders, 2018

Opinion of medical stakeholders according to different phases of infarction care	**Influencing factors which support access to health care**	**Influencing factors which barrier access to health care**
Pre-hospital care	Quick diagnosis with transtelephonic ECG (TTECG) in ambulance car. Optimal territorial coverage of ambulance care.	Weaknesses in education of patients: long hesitation time of asking for medical help. Bad road conditions in some places.
Hospitalization 1 (emergency care, cardiac catheterization, invasive acute cardiological care)	Effective cooperation between ambulance care and emergency care. New PCI centre after 2013 (percutaneous coronary intervention) could increase short-time survival chance.	Lack of capacity. Quick and successful cardiac catheterization worsened ill awareness of patients.
Hospitalization 2 (rehabilitation in hospital)	Effective professional cooperations based on progressivity. New professional protocols in rehabilitation.	Deficit in human resources. Lack of institutional network of health promotion.
Post-hospital care	Easy way to maintain health conditions after infarction at primary health care.	Weak compliance between doctors and patients. Overload primary health care.

Data source: Semi-structured interviews (n = 24) made with medical stakeholders (doctors, nurses, dietetists, physiotherapists etc.) in different health care institutions in Gyula, Békés county, Hungary, 2018.

Ambulance care with its availability and response times is one of the most important health services in pre-hospital care, which is the first phase of infarction care before hospitalization. It is of an excellent standard in Békés County according to both professionals' and patients' opinion of those interviewed.

Table 4. The most important influencing factors in access to health care based on semi-structured interviews made with patients, 2018

Opinion of patients according to different phases of infarction care	Influencing factors which support access to health care	Influencing factors which barrier access to health care
Pre-hospital care	Quick ambulance arrivals also in peripheral places.	If infarction symptoms are not so typical patients do not ask for medical care for a long time (long hesitation time).
Hospitalization 1 (emergency care, cardiac catheterization, invasive acute cardiological care)	Quick revascularization and less trauma but decreasing individual sense of responsibility.	Lifestyle guidance is based on not so much effective information transfer.
Hospitalization 2 (rehabilitation in hospital)	Rehabilitation care is working well and it is based on good cooperation between medical workers and patients.	Many patients refuse rehabilitation care because they have to start their work as soon as possible. Rehabilitation care is not recommended for all patients.
Post-hospital care	Permanent contact with general practitioner at residence settlement.	Keep healthy lifestyle is so expensive. Many patients do not participate at control care because they live so far from health services.

Data source: Semi-structured interviews (n = 29) made with patients (who had infarction at least once in his/her lifetime) in different health care institutions in Gyula, Békés county, Hungary, 2018.

Firstly, smaller ambulance care stations work within the county therefore territorial coverage is better. Secondly, there is an effective communication between ambulance care and hospital emergency care based on using transtelephonic ECG (TTECG). Thirdly, realizing optimal territorial aspects in infarction care means that AMI patients from different parts of the county are not taken to the hospitl of Gyula but to the nearer PCI centres of Debrecen or Szeged. The main problems faced by pre-hospital care are coming from the lack of health knowledge of the population and poor coverage in certain areas of the county. It means that patients hesitate or delay for a long time before calling for medical assistance and these long hesitation times as delays can consequently reduce the successful outcome of delayed PCI intervention (time window is 120 minutes). Furthermore, the poorer road conditions of border and peripheral areas of the county can slow down the ambulance respones times.

There was a big step forward in the hospitalization of infarction care in Békés County after 2010. This was a result of the opening of a new PCI centre in Pándy Kálmán Hospital of Gyula in 2013. The new centre offered better and quicker access to infarction care. Thus, it can improve access to modern infarction care coordinating the cooperation facilities of infarction care with other hospitals within the county such as the towns of Orosháza and Békéscsaba. The new facility has helped to create a more conjoined professional framework and a feeling of teamwork within the county's hospitals (e.g., among emergency care, invasive cardiology care, rehabilitation cardiology care).

The efficient and modern percutaneous coronary intervention (PCI) organized locally has significantly increased survival chances, shortened recovery periods and resulted better living standards after infarction. On the other hand, the improvement in access to modern infarction care has weakened the personal responsibility. In other words, some patients are not understanding of their own personal health responsibilities. There are a certain number of patients who have no or poor of understanding of disease awareness. Better and more available heath care often creates as many problems as it solves in certain areas of the population. It can barrier to follow doctors' instructions with the result of poor compliance. Many patients are not able to change lifestyle permanently according to their more disadvantaged socio-economic (level of incomes) and/or socio-cultural conditions (health behaviour). This is one of the most important requirements for successful recovery and avoidance of the further infarction in the long term.

In the rehabilitation phase of infarction care there were determinative changes in the recent years. For instance, new professional rehabilitation protocol was introduced in Hungary (e.g., introducing modern lifestyle consultation). However, only few patients can access to this rehabilitation treatment, because:

- many patients refuse it in order to return to work as soon as possible,
- some of them live far from the rehabilitation centre of Pándy Kálmán Hospital in Gyula and they can not take the longer trips,
- Rehabilitation is not offered in some cases.

It is also informative that there is a lack of practitioners (e.g., dietetist, psychologist, physiotherapist etc.) in rehabilitation care in Békés County.

In the post-hospital phase of infarction care general practitioners (GP) have primary role in maintaining the general health of patients after infarction. All areas in Hungary have their on GP as the part of the primary health care. This is currently a very fortunate situation in the Hungarian health care system, however there is a massive shortfall in human resources within the health care. In addition, primary health care is not completed by the national institutional system of health promotion, because of the lack of capacity.

All quantitative results and all qualitative experiences of our case study organized in Békés County are good evidence upon which to make some proposals which can be useful for local health care system and can reasonably be generalized nationally to identify further areas and barriers in access to health care.

It is also necessary to create and develop opportunities for integrated health care in Hungary as well as in Békés County in the near future. It could vertically contribute raising and strengthening the progressivity between certain health care levels while it could horizontally assist in more successful cooperation and links between health care institutions in certain parts of Békés County as well as Hungary. More focus on prevention and health promotion can help to improve the level of health knowledge within the general population. It can also help to reduce the life-threatening delays (hesitation times) in pre-hospital care. Quicker calls for medical assistance can provide a much higher chance of survival especially in those parts of the country which are more distant from hospitals and health care providers. Institutional and sectoral developing of patient education could promote the transformation of health behaviour and the realization of individual attitude's changing. To make these plans successful it is necessary to finance and develop better health services which are more commonly available. To improve long term chance of survival, it is imperative to have successful rehabilitation care. This can better support for permanent lifestyle changes in the long-term. GPs will have to take more high-profile role in these efforts especially in those communities which are further away from larger cities or health care centres. One of the possibilities is to extend the general family practice partnership in Hungary especially via non-medical net. In other words, it should:

- have stronger professional cooperation between GPs and other specialists/medical professionals (e.g., cardiologist, internist),
- coordinate their medical tasks in organizing patient pathways,
- complete effectively GP's work with the professional community of non-medical net (e.g., dietetist, psychologist, physiotherapist).

Moreover it could promote the integration of more communities primary health care with utilizing human resources and the optimal arrangements of services.

The expansion of institutional system of health promotion – e.g., founding new health promotion offices – can increase the influence of individual-made practical advice together with paying more attention to individuals' socio-economic and socio-cultural circumstances. It has a specific urban-rural relation because local conditions and social norms of healthy lifestyle are completely differ from each other in urban and rural areas.

Majority of all results and experiences of our case study could strengthen that difficulties in access to health care is one of determinative factors in health inequalities. Equity or inequity in access to health care can directly or indirectly influence socio-economic and socio-cultural components of health inequality and its regional distribution. Generally, an increased scale of health inequality has built up in Hungary during the recent years and can be detected according to demographic distribution (especially among women) and to spatial distribution. The improving health conditions and better access to modern cardiological care means considerably better survival chances, but a reduction in the individual health responsibility of the population.

The following section of this chapter is presenting the role of health policy in the emergence of health inequalities in Hungary and the barriers of access to health care. Defining the role of health policy content-analysis was used to analyse Hungarian health strategy planning through its primary documents.

THE EMERGENCE OF HEALTH INEQUALITY AND BARRIERS IN ACCESS TO HEALTH CARE IN THE HUNGARIAN HEALTH POLICY AND HEALTH STRATEGY PLANNING

The operational problems in the Hungarian health care system have been tried to be resolved by national health policy after the political and economic regime change in 1989. The problems were diverse: e.g., financing (simultaneous lack of resources and waste), obsolete old unsuitable buildings, outdated medical equipment, then later the lack of human resources and modern technology. The transformation process was called firstly health care reform, and later as structural transformation (Orosz, 2003). This is still happening today, as many of these problems simply could not be solved. The reform process consists of a series of measures and strategic planning that supports it. Thus, numerous laws and plans have been prepared, in which health policy goals and values appear.

Based on the content-analysis of health care policy documents, strategic plans and specific legislation, as well as health policy experts' declarations and other comprehensive overviews and reports, we can say that the equal access to health care, spatial justice or equal opportunity are reflected in connection with the transformation of health care system in Hungary. This can be observed both directly and indirectly too.

The emergence of equal access to health care system throughout the whole process is contradictory, as a sort of duality can be observed. This means that the fair access to the health care system (as a goal to be achieved) is phrased as value, on the other hand, they desire to solve the lack of resources by rationalizing capacities. The latter implies that certain forms of health care can be taken further away from the patients' residences. In many cases, the stated objective of a measure was, for example, to improve the health care of peripheral regions, but at the time of implementation, it was hardly improved, or possibly deteriorated and also the access to it. Thus, the range of forms of health care that can be taken locally or in the vicinity has narrowed. The consequence is that the two principles (justice and capacity reduction) in many cases conflict with each other.

It may also be the case that with increasing efficiency (e.g., reorganizing patient paths, introducing a volume limit of particular institutions) is intended to ensure more equal, equitable access. In this case, the logic of the measures is that if the system will be more efficient overall, it will result in better care for everyone. These ideas – if they became measures – could not achieve the two goals at the same time. Thus, in spite of the appearance of equal spatial access to health care as a goal, the outcome of the measures in many cases evoked the opposite effect.

In strategic health planning documents – over the past two and a half decades in Hungary – a shift in focus can also be observed. Firstly, the main goal was to increase efficiency, and then to ensure equal access. In certain cases, one or the other principle either came to prominence hidden (implicitly) or openly (explicitly). This should be illustrated through some examples.

Aiming to recognize the local needs and planning on a smaller geographic scale, in 1997 the Health Act was passed, within the Regional Modernization Program was launched in Hungary. This strengthened the decentralization of decisions in healt policy. The program was stopped in 1998, and centralization and efficiency were once again at the forefront.

Another important measure was the Law of CXXXII in 2006 about the development of the health care system. Almost all of the legislation deals with the rationalization of specialized care, basically in a territorial approach: in fact, a new territorial structure of national hospital beds and capacities has been developed. In some areas of the country, there were too many hospitals, but in others the inpatient care was inadequate. According to the principle of progressive care, the complex medical interventions requiring great expertise were centred in well-equipped, major hospitals and clinics in a way that from most settlements they can be reached within one hour. In addition, a smaller, so-called regional hospitals network has been formed, which can be reached within a 30-kilometer radius and provide basic care. In addition, the territorial care obligation was tightened (Uzzoli, 2007). As a result of the measures, the population organized demonstrations in several locations to maintain the current institutions.

These protests have led to increase territorial justice in the later measures. With the help of the European Union funding sources, an attempt has been made to improve outpatient care in deprived areas, and the number of ambulance stations was increased.

In 2012, the hospital capacity was reduced again, but no hospital was closed down like in 2006. At the same time, the territorial care obligation and the territorial assignment have been transformed deeper than ever. The goal was now a more powerful than ever spatial centralization of more specialized care. Specialized care tasks were divided into basic, middle and upper levels by specialization. Each hospital was assigned its specialization, specifying which tasks could be completed and the municipalities were assigned to them. Thus, a hospital did not have a single, but very wide service area, and the residents have had to go to various hospitals with various illnesses.

In 2010, the 'Semmelweis Plan' (2010-2014) and in 2014, the 'Healthy Hungary Plan' (2014-2020) have already declared that equal access is a priority, including specifics. This may be related to the fact that the Hungarian health care development strategy has to come closer to international standards, especially to the principles formulated by the European Union. In addition to equal access, however, both plans attempt to increase efficiency. On this basis, it can be stated that the Hungarian policy strategy planning and health policy have always tried to orient the development of health care by simultaneously maintaining these two often contradictory principles.

The following section of this chapter focuses on presenting the conclusions of this research highlighting the most important contradictions regarding access to health care in Hungary.

Conclusion

The primary aim of our empirical research was to interpret the role of access to health care in changes of health inequalities in Hungary in the terms of space and time after the change of regime of 1989. This was methodologically based on the statistical analysis of the morbidity and mortality data of the acute myocardial infarction and the empirical study of the operating mechanisms of the infarction care as the part of cardiology. All results and the experiences can be used to partly theoretical, partly empirical development of similar studies or to interpret the characteristics of health care of other noncommunicable diseases with significance in public health.

There is no doubt that the rate of death caused by infarction in Hungary has been significantly reduced over the last decade and a half, but the improvement has partly been accompanied by an increase in regional inequalities, which is mainly due to the increasing death of women. Further studies are needed to show that this growth can be explained by the health effects of the 2008/2009 economic crisis.

It should be noted that the number of PCI centres in Hungary has increased steadily since the early 2000s, which has improved the conditions of access to cardiac catheterization. However, the increase in regional inequalities in recent years raises the question of what other socio-economic factors may be a barrier to the opportunities of access to health care. It is also apparent from the interpretation of the controversial situation that, for example, how infarct mortality is related to the professional content and compliance of medical guidelines, rehabilitation, or the lifestyle and socio-economic circumstances of the patients (Belicza et al., 2016). Other research has confirmed that the 365-day infarction-mortality in Hungary as the long-term survival chances have worsened slightly after 2014 (MÉRTÉK, 2017).

Determining the chances of access to health care requires the use of quantitative and qualitative methods together. Statistical methods make it difficult to study the role of the individual (e.g., lifestyle) and institutional factors (such as patient path management) in defining inequalities and barriers in access to health care. This is why we have analysed the barrier and support factors of access through the technique of interviewing in a local case study.

Interviews with local health professionals in infarction care and patients diagnosed with infarction revealed the importance of access-related approaches to institutional-objective and individual-subjective approaches, as well as reveal contradictions that could be identified by opinions. Numerous experiences have substantiated the hypothesis that in many cases, professional measures supporting access (e.g., medical guidelines) and investment (e.g., infrastructure development) are understood by health care professionals as an opportunity to access, but the patients perceived them only partially a better chance to access. This finding is also true in the reverse: patients believe that there are more opportunities to develop in the future to help access to health care, but these conditions are less pronounced in the opinion of health care providers. For example, new care protocols have been introduced in rehabilitation in recent years, mainly based on professional coordination in lifestyle counseling, but patients more prefer personalized advice.

Both health care professionals and patients agreed that the focus should be more on patient education, awareness-raising, and prevention programs in Hungary in the future. It is commonly seen that patients are unable to recognize the symptoms of an infarction, and are unsure whether they need to go to a doctor with an atypical syndrome. This problem also appears on the side of the health care system, because the later the cardiac catheterization (e.g., over the 120-minute time window) will result worse survival chances. This problem has already been demonstrated by previous research, highlighting the importance of reducing the pre-hospital delay time (Jánosi et al., 2017). Medical studies analywing the role of socio-economic factors influencing the possibilities of access to health care have already drawn attention to the need to patient education (e.g., Márk et al., 2015), the importance of secondary prevention treatments (e.g., Dani et al., 2018), and the role of the health behavior of patients in ill-awareness (e.g., Márk et al., 2018).

There is also a consensus between health care providers and patients on the fact that the institutional background of health promotion is weak in Hungary. There is a deficit in human resources of medical professional, public health services are lacking in small settlements, and general practitioners are less able to undertake preventive tasks due to their overload.

The widespread provision of equal opportunities and the reduction of health inequalities has become a priority for health policy decision-making at both the global and national level. In Hungary, a decisive goal in the hub of post-1989 health policy ambitions is to improve the health conditions of the population, to enhance primary and secondary prevention, and to strengthen primary health care. The main goals and tasks are grouped around a few key principles:

- Ensuring effectiveness in health care through mainstreaming health equity.
- Increasing efficiency in health care by streamlining health care tasks.

Creating and developing the conditions for access to health care primarily supports the achievement of effectiveness, but can also contribute to improving efficiency.

In the next phase of our research project the most relevant tasks will be to work out the empirical framework of synthesize the most informative results and experiences of the whole research. These scientific activities will also contain the method of making expert interviews. This will reveal some essential information about the process of decision-making from the point of view of policy decision-makers. All of these outputs based on making expert interviews can contribute to draw up decisive recommendations for decision-makers to reduce health inequalities regarding access to health care in Hungary. These recommendations also help to develop the conditions of the evidence based health policy.

References

Almeida, A. P. S. C. et al. 2017. Socioeconomic determinants of access to health services among older adults: A systematic review. *Revista de Saúde Pública* 51(50): doi: 10.1590/S1518-8787.2017051006661.

Andersen, R. M. 1995. Revisiting the behavioral model and access to medical care: does It matter? *Journal of Health and Social Behavior* 36(1): 1–10.

Belicza, É. and Jánosi, A. 2012. A heveny szívinfarktus előfordulásának és ellátásának vizsgálata a finanszírozási adatbázis elemzésével: 2004-2009. [Examination of financial database of infarction care: 2004-2009] *Orvosi Hetil*ap 153(3): 102–112.

Belicza, É. and Lám, J. and Kósa, I. 2016. Az acut myocardialis infarctus főbb hazai ellátási jellemzői 2005–2009 között az EuroHOPE kutatás eredményei alapján. [Some features of infarction care in Hungary based on EuroHOPE reserach.] *Orvosi Hetilap* 157(41): 1626–1634.

Beke, Sz. 2017. Békés megye népessége az egészségi állapot tükrében. [Health status in Békés county.] *Egészségtudomány* (3): 57–74.

Békés Megye Integrált Területi Programja 2014–2020. [*Integrated Regional Plan of Békés County 2014–2020.*] Békéscsaba: Békés Megyei Önkormányzat. 2015.

Braveman, P. A. 2003. Monitoring Equity in Health and Healthcare: A Conceptual Framework. *Journal of Health, Population and Nutrition* 21(3):181–192.

Cornia, G. A. and Paniccia, R. 2000. *The Transition Mortality Crisis: Evidence, Interpretation and Policy Responses.* New York: Oxford University Press.

Dani, Gy. and Blidár, T. and Márk, L. (2018): A szekunder prevenciós kezelések fontossági sorrendje a betegek szemében. [Importance of secondary preventive care for patients.] *Metabolizmus* 16(1): 50–54.

Daniels, N. 1982. Equity of Access to health care: Some conceptual and ethical issues. *The Milbank Memorial Fund Quarterly* 60:51–81.

Donabedian, A. 1973. *Aspects of medical care administration.* Cambridge: Harvard University Press.

Donabedian, A. 1990. The seven pillars of quality. *Archives of Pathology and Laboratory Medicine* 114(11):1115–1118.

Egészséges Magyarország Terv 2014-2020. Egészségügyi Ágazati Stratégia. [Healthy Hungary Plan 2014-2020. Health Sectoral Strategy.] Budapest: EMMI. 2014.

Egri, Z. and Tánczos, T. 2015. Socio-Economic and Spatial Correlations of the Eastern European Health Paradox in Hungary. Retrieved from *Deturope – The Central European Journal of Regional Development and Tourism* (7)2.

Egri, Z. 2016. Magyarország városai közötti egészségegyenlőtlenségek. [Health inequalities among the Hungarian cities.] *Területi Statisztika,* 57(5): 537–575.

Gaál, P. et al. 2011. Hungary – Health system review. Health Systems in Transition. *European Observatory on Health Systems and Policies* 13(5).

Gulliford, M. et al. 2002. What does 'access to health care' mean? *Journal of Health Services Research and Policy* 7(3): 186–188.

Hagen, T. P. et al. 2015. Acute Myocardial Infarction, Use of Percutaneous Coronary Intervention, and Mortality: A Comparative Effectiveness Analysis Covering Seven European Countries. *Health Economics* 24(2): 88–101.

Health Statistical Yearbooks of Hungary 1989–2016. Budapest: Hungarian Central Statistical Office.

Jánosi, A. et al. 2017. A szívinfarktus miatt kezelt betegek ellá-tása Magyarországon. *Orvosi Hetilap* 158(3): 90–93. [Treatment of patients treated for heart attack in Hungary. *Medical Weekly*]

Johnston, R. J. et al. 2000. *The Dictionary of Human Geography.* Oxford: Blackwell Publish Ltd.

Jones, K. and Moon, G. 1987. *Health, Disease and Society: A Critical Medical Geography.* New York: Routledge & Kegan Paul Ltd.

Józan, P. 1994a. Epidemiológiai válság Magyarországon a kilencvenes években I. [Epidemiological crisis in Hungary in the 1990s I.] *Statisztikai Szemle* 72 (1–2): 5–20.

Józan, P. 1994b. Epidemiológiai válság Magyarországon a kilencvenes években II. [Epidemiological crisis in Hungary in the 1990s II.] *Statisztikai Szemle* 72(3–4): 101–113.

Józan, P. 1996. Changes in Mortality in Hungary between 1980 and 1994. *Atlantic Studies on Societies in Change* 85: 111–138.

Kemkers, R. and Pirisi, G. and Trócsányi, A. 2010. A mentőellátás területi jellemzői Magyarországon. [Ambulance care in Hungary.] *Területi Statisztika* 50(4): 420–437.

Kiss, É. 2016. Területi különbségek a hazai népesség egészségi állapotában, 1989 után. [Regional differences in health in Hungary after 1989.] *Területi Statisztika* 56(5): 483–519.

Kiss, J. P. and Mattányi, Zs. 2005. *Stroke-ellátó központok és körzeteik optimalizálása a legrövidebb eljutási idő alapján.* [Optimalization of stroke care centres and its surroundings based on the best availability.] Retrieved from http://geogr.elte.hu/REF/REF_Cikkek/KJP_Kiss-Matt%C3%A1nyi%20Sopron%20-%20STROKE.pdf.

Kiss, J. P. 2013. A hazai egészségügyi szakellátások területi kérdései. [Regional dimensions of specialized medical care in Hungary.] In: Ember, I. and Pál, V. and Tóth, J. (Eds.): *Egészségföldrajz.* [*Geography of Health.*] 393–426. Budapest: Medicina Könyvkiadó Zrt.

Kovai, C. 2017. Az etnicitás szerepe az egészségegyenlőtlenségek magyarázatában, és a hozzáférés esélyei a magyarországi hátrányos helyzetű csoportoknál. [The role of ethnicity in health inequalities, and the chances of access to health care among disadvantaged social groups in Hungary.] In: Torgyik, J. (Ed.): *Válogatott tanulmányok a társadalomtudományok köréből.* [*Some selected papers from social sciences.*] 227–236. Komárno: International Research Institute (IRI).

Kovács, P. and Pirisi, G. and Trócsányi, A. 2013. Az egészségügyi alapellátó és sürgősségi rendszer területi képe Magyarországon. [Spatial pattern of primary and emergency health care in Hungary.] In: Ember, I. and Pál, V. and Tóth, J. (Eds.): *Egészségföldrajz.* [*Geography of Health.*] 378–392. Budapest: Medicina Könyvkiadó Zrt.

Kovács, K. and Tóth, G. 2015. Egészségi állapot. (Health status.) In: Monostori, J. and Őri, P. and Spéder, Zs. (Eds.): *Demográfiai portré*

2015. [*Demography portait 2015.*] 95–114. Budapest: KSH Népességtudományi Kutatóintézet.

Levesque, J. F. and Harris, M. F. and Russell, G. 2013. Patient-centred access to health care: conceptualising access at the interface of health systems and populations. *International Journal for Equity in Health* 12(18): 1–9.

Márk, L. et al. 2015. Változott-e a szívinfarktus prehospitális ideje és kezdetének napszaki ingadozása az elmúlt negyed évszázadban a gyulai kórház ellátási területén? [Did pre-hospital time of infarction change during the last 25 years in the surroundings of the hospital of Gyula ?] *Cardiologia Hungarica* 45(253): 253–257.

Márk, L. et al. 2018. Akut coronariaszindróma miatt 2015-ben kezelt betegeink lipidcsökkentő terápiája. [Our patients who were cared by statins regarding acute coronary syndroms.] *Orvosi Hetilap* 159(12): 478–484.

MÉRTÉK 2017. *Fókuszterület: Szívinfarktus-ellátás.* [*In focus: infarction care.*] Budapest: ÁEEK.

Napier, A. D. et al. 2017. *Culture matters: using a cultural contexts of health approach to enhance policy-making*. Policy brief, No. 1. WHO. 54 p.

NKFIA, 2016. *Az egészségügyi ellátáshoz való hozzáférés szerepe az egészségegyenlőtlenségekben Magyarországon.* [*The role of access to health care in health inequalities in Hungary*]. Budapest: NKFIH – K 119574. Retrieved from https://egeszsegugyihozzaferhetoseg.wordpress.com/.

Omran, A. R. 2005. "The epidemiological transition: A theory of the epidemiology of population change". *The Milbank Quarterly* 83(4): 731–57, doi:10.1111/j.1468-0009.2005.00398.x Reprinted from *The Milbank Memorial Fund Quarterly* 1971. 49(4): 509–538.

Orosz, É. 2003. Egészség és egészségügy az ezredfordulón. [Health and health care at millennium.] In: Kulcsár, K. – Bayer, J. (Eds.): *Társadalom, politika, jogrend.* [*Society, policy, law*] Magyar Tudománytár 4. 177 – 209. Budapest: MTA Társadalomkutató Központ – Kossuth Kiadó.

Orosz, É. 2013. Az egészségügyi rendszerek kihívásai a gazdasági válság időszakában. [Challenges for health care systems during crisis periods.] *Egészségügyi Gazdasági Szemle* 51(1): 1–11.

Orosz, É. and Kollányi, Zs. 2016. Egészségi állapot, egészség-egyenlőtlenségek nemzetközi összehasonlításban. [Health and health inequalities in international comparison.] In: Kolosi, T. and Tóth, I. Gy. (Eds.): *Társadalmi Riport* 2016. [*Social Report 2016.*] 334–357. Budapest: TÁRKI.

Pál, V. 2017. Egészségünk földrajza – területi különbségek a hazai egészségi állapotban. [Geography of health – Regional differences in health in Hungary.] *Magyar Tudomány* 178(3): 311–321.

Penchansky, R. and Thomas, W. J. 1981. The concept of access: definition and relationship to consumer satisfaction. *Medical Care* 19(2):127–140.

Regional Statistical Yearbooks of Hungary 1989–2016. Budapest: Hungarian Central Statistical Office.

Semmelweis Terv az egészségügy megmentésére 2010-2014. Újraélesztett egészségügy – Gyógyuló Magyarország. [Semmelweis Plan for saving health care. Revivication of health care – healing Hungary 2010-2014] Budapest: EMMI. 2010.

Skrabski, Á. and Kopp, M. and Kawachi, I. 2003. Social capital in a changing society: cross sectional associations with middle aged female and male mortality rates. *Journal of Epidemiology and Community Health* 57(2): 114-119.

Skrabski, Á. and Kopp, M. and Kawachi, I. 2004. Social capital and collective efficacy in Hungary: cross sectional associations with middle aged female and male mortality rates. *Journal of Epidemiology and Community Health*, 58(1): 340–345.

Statistical Yearbooks of Hungary 1989–2016. Budapest: Hungarian Central Statistical Office.

Tariq, S. and Woodman, J. 2013. Using Mixed Methods in Health Research. *Journal of the Royal Society of Medicine Short Reports* 4. Retrieved from http://dx.doi.org/10.1177/2042533313479197.

The Global Health 50/50 Report 2018. London: University College. Retrieved from https://globalhealth5050.org/report/.

Tóth, G. et al. 2018. Az egészségügyi ellátáshoz való hozzáférés szerepe az egészségegyenlőtlenségekben – A szívizominfarktus-megbetegedések és -halálozások területi különbségei. [Role of access to health care in health inequalities – Morbidity and mortality of infarction and its regional differences.] *Területi Statisztika* 58(4): 346–379.

Uzzoli, A. 2007. A magyar egészségügyi ellátórendszer strukturális átalakításának területi vonatkozásai. [Territorial aspects of structural changes in the Hungarian health care system.] *Tér és Társadalom* 21(3): 103–115.

Uzzoli, A. 2011. The role of unemployment in the run of life chances in Hungary. *International Journal of Population Research* 2011/1. doi:10.1155/2011/130318 Retrieved from http://www.hindawi.com/journals/ijpr/2011/130318.html.

Uzzoli, A. 2016. Health inequalities regarding territorial differences in Hungary by discussing life expectancy. *Regional Statistics* 1: 139–163.

Vitrai, J. et al. 2008. *Egészségegyenlőtlenségek Magyarországon – Adatok az ellátási szükségletek térségi egyenlőtlenségeinek becsléséhez. [Health inequalities in Hungary – Data for estimation of regional differences in supply needs.]* Budapest: EgészségMonitor Kutató és Tanácsadó Nonprofit Közhasznú Kft.

Waters, H. R. 2000. Measuring equity in access to health care. *Social Science and Medicine* 51:599–612.

Whitehead, M. 1992. The concepts and principles of equity and health. *International Journal of Health Service* 22(3): 429–445.

Wilkinson, R. G. 1996. *Unhealthy Societies: The Afflictions of Inequality*. London: Routledge.

Wisdom, J. and Creswell, J. W. 2013. *Mixed Methods: Integrating Quantitative and Qualitative Data Collection and Analysis While Studying Patient-Centered Medical Home Models.* AHRQ Publication No: 13-0028-EF https://pcmh.ahrq.gov/page/mixed-methodsintegrating-quantitative-and-qualitative-data-collection-and-analysis-while Retrieved on 31 October 2018.

www.ksh.hu.

www.webofknowledge.com.

www.who.int.

Biographical Sketch

Annamaria Uzzoli

Affiliation: Institute for Regional Studies, Centre for Economic and Regional Studies, Hungarian Academy of Sciences, Budapest, Hungary

Education: PhD in Earth Sciences (Human Geography)

Research and Professional Experience: Studies in Geography of Health (health inequalities, access to health care, regional disparities of health)

Professional Appointments: PhD, Senior research fellow.

Publications from the Last 3 Years:

1. Egedy, T., Uzzoli, A. 2016. Cities as the keys to survival? – The impact of the economic crisis on health inequalities in Hungary in terms of unemployment and life expectancy. *Urbani Izziv* 27(2): 97–111.
2. Uzzoli, A. 2016. Health inequalities regarding territorial differences in Hungary by discussing life expectancy. *Regional Statistics* (1): 139–163.
3. Király, G., Czirfusz, M., Koós, B., Tagai, G., Uzzoli, A. 2017. Population projection for Hungary and its relation with climate change. *Europa XXI* 32(1): 5–20.
4. Uzzoli, A. 2017. Hungarian health inequalities regarding accessibility. IRI Conference on Culture, Society, Responsibility. In: Tibor Janos Karlovitz (ed.): *Selected Papers from Responsibility*. International Research Institute, Komarno, Slovakia. pp. 48–54.

5. Uzzoli, A. 2018. Health inequalities and access to health care in urban areas – A case study in Budapest, Hungary. In: Trzepacz, Piotr – Warchalska-Troll, Agatha (Eds.): *East Meets West – Contemporary Urban Issues Revisited. 2nd International Conference of the Urban Development Issues Journal.* Book of Abstracts. National Institute for Spatial Policy and Housing, Crakow, Poland. p. 24.

In: An In Depth Look at Hungary
Editor: Esperanta Rompa
ISBN: 978-1-53615-351-4

Chapter 2

FEATURES OF THE HUNGARIAN TEACHER EDUCATION SYSTEM

Katinka Bacskai*[1]*, PhD, Veronika Bocsi*[2,*]*, PhD, Ágnes Engler*[1]*, PhD and Gabriella Pusztai*[1]*, PhD

[1]Faculty of Arts, University of Debrecen, Hajdúböszörmény, Hungary
[2]Faculty of Education for Children and Special Education Needs, University of Debrecen, Hajdúböszörmény, Hungary

ABSTRACT

The study aims to give an overview of the Hungarian teacher education system. We describe the social and cultural features of the country and the main parameters of the Hungarian education system (e.g., the relationship between social mobility and education). We try to give an adequate framework by which the system of teacher education can be interpreted. The presentation of the teacher education program includes a short historical overview. The Bologna Process and its subsequent modifications are also analyzed. Our aim is to describe the present features of different types of training programs and institutions. Teacher education students' socio-cultural background is also investigated. This is a very

* Corresponding Author's Email: bocsiveron@gmail.com.

important issue because students from a disadvantaged background are generally overrepresented in teacher education.

During the past fifteen years, several circumstances have changed in the system of teacher education (aptitude test, training set-up, the curriculum of training programs, special scholarship programs for students, teaching practice). We try to list these important changes and analyze their potential and direct effects.

Keywords: teacher education, education system, Hungary, disadvantaged children

Introduction

Our study aims to give an overview of the Hungarian teacher education system. For reasons of space, we are unable to provide a thorough description, therefore we intend to explore the cardinal questions of the Hungarian teacher education system by highlighting certain aspects. First, we describe the connection between education and society, and then we report the social background and historical transformation of teacher education, including major trends after the Millennium and differences by the types of organizations which run the institutions. In the second chapter, we outline teachers' and teacher education students' characteristics, then explore the possibilities of disadvantaged children's special care. We also present an overview of how some institutions put this special care into practice and how they enable disadvantaged students to connect with other students.

Education, Society and Teacher Education

Characteristics and Social Embeddedness of the Hungarian Education System

Arguably, the most important questions of education sociology regard the complicated relationship between education institutions and social inequalities. It is vital to ask whether the education system is able to reduce inequalities, and if it is, to what extent; whether it reinforces or opens the closed structure of society; and whether it can be a channel for mobility. The education system as a whole can only be investigated thoroughly in a given social space and time. It is important to see that the social mobility function of education is influenced by various factors such as the traditions of the education system or the employed education methodology. The mobility rate and basic structure of society also offer essential context. This mechanism of operation is affected by education policy decisions as well as the process of education expansion.

The theoretical background of our educational overview is centered around the expansion of education, which reached secondary education in Hungary in the 1970s and higher education around the Millennium. Recently, the literature has already started to explore the stagnation of higher education expansion in Hungary (Híves & Kozma 2014), which is due to demographic developments and changes in education policy, mainly affecting part time students' number and proportion. Inequalities and mobility opportunities display new divisions since the introduction of the Bologna Process in higher education (Hrubos 2002, Veroszta 2016), while diversification has caused divergence in the status of faculties and institutions.

Hungarian education sociology studies often analyze the strong social embeddedness of education efficiency (Szemerszki 2015), which is impacted by structural differences in education and the various types of organizations which run the institutions. Family background and school environment also influence academic efficiency. School choice is often determined by distinct enrolment strategies of parents from different social backgrounds, although the effect of school environment can be shown independently. The literature has yet to reach consensus regarding its size, however (Bacskai 2015). The social and institutional embeddedness of efficiency is also studied in higher education (see Pusztai & Kovács 2015). The education system in Hungary as a whole is selective (Csapó, Molnár & Kinyó 2009).

Although Hungarian society has been characterized by rising wealth inequality since the fall of communism, both the difference between the lowest and highest deciles and the GINI coefficient imply moderate inequality in European comparison (Eurostat 2018). Hungarian society displays low mobility and isolation between different groups, as shown by European (Eurofund 2017) and Hungarian studies (Csepeli 2016). Isolation between groups might be reinforced by the relatively selective education system, which could be diminished through well-targeted education policy measures, however.

Demographic trends show that teachers should expect an increase in the number of deprived children. In younger age cohorts, the proportion of those who live in poverty is substantially higher (I4). Roma population in Hungary comprises 8-9 percent of society. Roma children are overrepresented in the Eastern and Northern areas as well as in the Southern Transdanubia region. The proportion of Roma pupils in some counties is estimated to have exceeded 30% (Papp Z. 2011).

History of Hungarian Teacher Education

After describing the social background of education, we turn to the history and present state of teacher education.

The history of primary and secondary teacher education is a well-documented field within Hungarian education history. Nevertheless, many researchers study primary and secondary education separately, with little overlap in their analyses. Nagy (2004) has pointed out the apparent professionalization of the two fields. Differences between primary and secondary teacher education become evident early on: primary teacher education is practice-oriented, whereas secondary teacher education is dominated by academic and theoretical elements.

Until the mid-20th century, most schools were run by churches, which meant that curricula were set by different denominations. In the second half of the 19th century, teacher education institutions which were independent of denominations began to appear: 1869 marked the establishment of the first teacher education institution run by the state (Kelemen 2007). The 1777 act called Ratio Education is regulated teacher education requirements. Teacher education started as a mere course then moved to the secondary level by the second half of the 19th century. At teacher education institutions, disciplinary education was provided by universities, while the necessary practice could be acquired in special schools of teaching practice. These schools were often established to provide teaching practice to teacher education students (Brezsnyánszky & Fenyő 2009).

Similar to other countries in Central Europe, Hungary went through a Soviet-style transformation with communists taking power in 1947, which caused fundamental changes in the education system. The new regime held both teacher education faculties and methodology training specialists in low regard. Political transformation was accompanied by primary and secondary teacher education institutions being taken over from church oversight to state control. Programs integrated into universities prepared students to teach in secondary schools, while colleges trained students to become primary school teachers. Kindergarten teachers and primary school teachers of pupils in years 1 to 4 were educated in a separate tertiary program.

The duration of teaching practice had barely changed since the 19th century: secondary school teachers taught the fewest practice classes, followed by primary school teachers, with kindergarten teachers having the most practice. The fall of communism in 1989 did not bring about substantial changes in the system of teacher education. However, a major transition began in the 2000s with the expansion of higher education, which resulted in a large increase in the number of applicants. Due to the absence of examinations upon admission, many graduates did not find employment as teachers or taught at a level of education different from their training (Hunyady 2010a).

Teacher Education after the Millennium

Due to its embeddedness into higher education, teacher education in Hungary mirrored the institutional changes of higher education. The fall of communism at the turn of the 1980s and 1990s accelerated international processes which had been long on the table in international higher education discourse. For decades, many had called for and expected the integration of higher education, student and faculty mobility, a standardized credit transfer and accumulation system, which became possible through the opening of borders. The reform process began with the Magna Charta Universitatum (1988) and the Sorbonne Joint Declaration (1998) and reached its peak in the Bologna Declaration with the aim of a single higher education area (see Hrubos 2002, Kozma & Rébay 2008, Hunyady 2010b, Szolár 2010, Rónay 2018).

Among the measures in the Bologna Declaration, teacher education was affected the most by the introduction of the two-cycle tertiary education. Before the Bologna Process, teacher education in Hungary was offered in undivided programs at two different tertiary institution types. Colleges trained primary school teachers, with some of them eligible to teach in the first four years and others in the second four years of primary school. The duration of the program was four years, and teaching practice started early on. College training for primary school teachers followed practice-oriented curricula with a special emphasis on methodology. At universities, those who wished to become secondary school teachers could join the program after one year of education in their field (or fields) of specialization. Thus, four of their five university years were spent in both disciplinary education and teacher training. Along with subjects related to methodology, curricula also featured theoretical courses about the field of study extensively. Students began to familiarize themselves with the environment of schools one year (or one and a half years) after their admission and completed their teaching practice in the last year of the program. Their degree enabled them to teach in secondary schools and in the final years of bachelor's programs. In the 1990s, some posed the question whether qualifications to teach at lower and upper secondary levels should be differentiated (in the form of bachelor's and master's degrees) (Szabó 1998). The number of students in Hungary increased steadily in the expansion process which started in the first half of the 1990s, accompanied by the unwavering popularity of teacher education. However, many graduates of teacher education chose to seek employment outside the education system.

The introduction of the two-cycle tertiary education in 2006 meant that the main component of teacher education became part of master's programs. (By contrast, kindergarten teachers, lower primary school and remedial teachers could start working after receiving their bachelor's degree.) A new component, a half-year external teaching practice supervised by a mentor teacher, was also introduced. Students could take courses in the field of pedagogy or psychology for their minor to advance their future teacher education. Some have noted that the changes were beneficial because university and college-level teacher training had been standardized with respect to duration, program supply, criteria. and output (Soósné 2010). At the same time, "teacher education at universities was under pressure from both the standardized criteria system and integration" (Brezsnyánszky 2006: 59). Problems arose from the unbalanced weighting of majors and minors and the strong presence of pedagogical courses. The changes also presupposed a dedication towards the teaching profession at the bachelor's level. The interdisciplinary nature of university education was weakened, the fields of pedagogy and psychology, however, grew in significance, which strengthened the competition between disciplinary and teacher training (Sáska 2015).

A further advantage of the new system of teacher education under the Bologna Process was the elimination of disadvantages which stemmed from the duality (university-college training) of the previous system (e.g., uniform program duration, degrees which allow teachers to work at specific levels of education). Bachelor's degrees provided more time to opt for the teaching profession and put a large emphasis on teaching practice (Pukánszky 2014).

The divided structure of teacher education sparked fierce debate which resulted in the termination of the Bologna system. In 2013, undivided teacher education was reintroduced, with slight modifications: primary school teachers are now trained for 4+1 years, while secondary school teachers study for 5+1 years, completing the same number of credits in both cases. The extra years mark the compulsory teaching practice at schools. More emphasis is laid on both pedagogical-psychological training and disciplinary education. The new system poses operational risks with respect to the long-run sustainability and professional accountability of the one-year-long teaching practice, and regarding the program duration in general. The latter issue might be problematic because more years are spent in education (which delays labor market entry) and disadvantaged students may attrite (Sáska 2015).

Teacher Education in the Non-Public Higher Education Sector

After the fall of communism, there have been significant changes in the number of different organizations which run educational institutions. In our study, we present the characteristics of church-run institutions in regards to teacher education.

In 2015, 7 of the 27 universities in Hungary were run privately, and 30 of the 40 colleges were private institutions. We characterize all institutions which are not run by the state as private. Among private higher education institutions church management dominates: as of 2015, 5 of the 7 private universities were run by a church, and 21 of the 30 private colleges were also run by different denominations, while the rest were maintained by non-profit and for-profit organizations.

According to cooperationist models of the relationship between church and state, denominations are not in need of separate higher education institutions (Schanda 2004). A version of this concept states that parallel denominational units may exist within the same state-run institution in any general scientific field, especially in the case of ideology-sensitive disciplines (philosophy, pedagogy, etc.). On the other hand, the theory arguing for separate church-run higher education institutions states that minority denominations, which were repressed for long years and may lack the access to state-run universities, are also entitled to train their own intellectual generation, that is, denominational institutions are needed in every area of tertiary education. Moreover, there are specific fields of training within the entire spectrum of qualifications which are particularly important for denominations because of their special social responsibility. These special fields also include teacher education.

In Hungary during the 1990s, denominations aimed to establish separate higher education institutions. As a result, both a Catholic and a Protestant university now have separate pedagogical faculties, and several colleges with pedagogical training have also been founded (Pusztai 2010). After the political transformation, one of the most important challenges of restructuring the education system was to ensure pluralism in education, after decades of domination by totalitarian ideology. During the past two and half decades, the number of church-run schools has increased, and demand for such institutions has been continuous (Pusztai 2006). Today more than one in every ten primary school pupils and one in every five secondary school students attend church-run schools. (Pusztai 2015, Bacskai-Pusztai 2015). Parents who choose these schools for their children expect teachers to play a broader role (Pusztai 2015). Our qualitative studies have shown that managers in church-run schools have higher expectations regarding teachers (Bocsi et al. 2015). The question can be raised whether teacher education is able to prepare future teachers to their broader role in the system.

Around 85% of church-run higher education institutions are very small, with less than 1,000 students. They serve mainly as theological institutions to supply different denominations with professionals, but they also train religious instruction teachers. Recently four BA programs, two MA programs and undivided 5-year teacher training programs are available for those who have chosen church-run institutions. In Hungary, there is no opportunity to study to become a remedial teacher at any church-run institution as all 5 such institutions are state-run. All other programs are available at institutions run by churches. At the BA level, church-run institutions offer degrees for students who would like to work as kindergarten teachers or primary school teachers. According to the Statistics of Higher Education Admission Information System, 4 of the 20 institutions preparing primary school teachers are church-run, while 4 of the 18 institutions training kindergarten teachers are maintained by a denomination, and only 1 is church-run of the 11 institutions which train infant and toddler teachers. Most religious higher education institutions offer the opportunity for students to study in undivided 5-year teacher training programs since 12 of 42 such institutions are church-run. If we analyze student ratios, we find that the proportion of students admitted to church-run primary school teacher training is less than 26 percent. Nearly 20 percent of kindergarten teachers study at church-maintained institutions. One in every ten future infant and toddler teachers studies at faith-based higher education institutions. The proportion of teacher education students preparing for ISCED 2 and 3 is relatively low, around 10 percent, in contrast with the increasingly important role of denominational schools.

The difference in the composition of the student body at church-run and state-run institutions is that the former group achieved on average a higher total score during the general higher education admission process. The difference comes mainly from students in church run teacher training programs, who tend to gain higher points on the entrance exam. It is particularly interesting that the proportion of non-Hungarian citizens is double at church-run higher education institutions than at state-run ones. Furthermore, we have examined the gender distribution of recently admitted students in public and private higher education based on admissions data. We have found a significant correlation, namely that women are more likely to participate in teacher education run by a church (87.4% as compared to 79%), and therefore the feminization at these institutions is even more pronounced.

Although there are separate public and private sectors in teacher education in Hungary, this has not brought about the pillarization of the job market for teachers. Pillarization means an institutional separation of groups in society based on denominations, as observed in the Netherlands and in France. In Hungary, denominational college and university graduates can be teachers in public schools. About 40% of denominational college and university graduates are employed in public schools and nearly 25% of public teacher education graduates work in denominational schools.

Teacher attrition is one of the most widespread problems in European education. The vast majority of graduates in church-run teacher training do not plan to leave the teaching profession, but there are significant differences between public and denominational higher education graduates with regard to their persistence in the profession since teacher retention is weaker in the public sector. Differences in the persistence to stay in the teacher profession could be explained by the different school climate of sectors. Since parental expectations towards teachers to transmit values differ significantly in denominational schools compared to public schools, the comparison of child-rearing values among teachers who are employed in different schools is an important topic. Studies indicate that graduates in church-run teacher education have considerably different child-rearing values than public graduates. Traditional, prosocial, collaborative, community values dominate their value system, which helps them develop a more favorable school climate. Perhaps it is this school climate which supports them to preserve their professional calling.

Teacher Education Students, Teachers and Students

In the second part of our study, after having explored the system of teacher education, we turn to its participants: teachers and teacher education students. As we have seen, Hungarian society has a relatively closed structure, with underprivileged students' absence becoming increasingly apparent. Thus, at the end of the chapter, we investigate disadvantaged children's education possibilities and characteristics.

The teaching profession has always been an important mobility path. Whereas teachers whose parents do not have a tertiary degree are overrepresented at education levels at which children are relatively young (e.g., in kindergarten or primary school teacher education – in Hungary, both kindergarten teachers and infant and toddler teachers are trained at the bachelor's level), at more advanced levels of education, especially in higher education, teachers from high-status families are in the majority. This relationship can be observed among teacher education students as well as practicing teachers. A Hungarian study has also pointed out that teachers often pass on their profession from one generation to the other, which might create so-called teacher dynasties (Pócsik 2015).

Hungarian teachers' social composition can be characterized by significant feminization (which exceeds the European average, and increases at lower ISCED levels) and an aging teacher community (Veroszta 2015). Problems stemming from aging teacher composition affect fields differently, with natural sciences impacted to a larger extent.

Regarding teacher education students, we can observe that those who come from a disadvantaged socio-cultural background, who receive extra admission points due to their underprivileged situation and who were born in a village are more likely to enter teacher education. Teacher education students' socio-economic background also varies across ISCED levels and disciplines.

The relatively low prestige of the teaching profession has been shown by multiple Hungarian analyses. Lannert (2010) has pointed out that Hungarian teachers' workload is close to the European average, while their subjective wellbeing is significantly below that. This implies that high-status applicants tend to not choose teacher education.

Due to the demographic trends mentioned above, recently graduated teachers are more likely to start their career at institutions with a high proportion of disadvantaged and Roma children. These regions are also characterized by a shortage of teachers with high fluctuations. Teachers are often employed without the necessary qualifications. The closed characteristics of Hungarian society also appear in the education system, resulting in the situation that teachers at primary and secondary institutions that accept students from disadvantaged backgrounds are required to have markedly different pedagogical methods. At the other end of the spectrum, a cluster of schools with high student efficiency and a large rate of further studies have emerged.

The expansion of tertiary education has also transformed the prestige and social base of certain institutions. Increasing differences in prestige have reinforced the low position of kindergarten and primary teacher education in the institutional hierarchy.

Teacher Education and Low SES Schools in Hungary

Hungarian and, more broadly, continental education is mostly teacher-centered: it is based on the cooperation between teacher and class. This structure can be applied in a frictionless manner in homogeneous classes where both the teacher and pupils value academic performance. In Hungary, selection among schools is increasingly prevalent, which results in more homogeneous school communities. Therefore some schools have the majority of students from a favorable socio-economic background, while, inevitably, school communities at other institutions regard academic performance less important since children there do not come typically from "middle-class" families. In the international literature, many studies have explored how teachers and institutions educate disadvantaged, poor, and low-status children. Burnet and Lampert (2011) have described the phenomenon in the terminology of sociology by calling these institutions "Low SES School Communities."

Although various studies suggest that primary school pupils' status is mostly determined by their parents' status, many significant findings have shown since the 1960s that the social composition of schools influences academic performance strongly (Coleman 1966). School composition has been also in the center of analyses which explore teachers' activities and their efficacy. The international literature uses various terms to describe institutions with a majority of students from below-average socio-economic status: hard-to-staff schools (Castro et al. 2010; Darling-Hammond 2010), most challenging schools (Rice 2008), at-risk schools (Castro et al. 2010; Darling-Hammond 2010), or disadvantaged schools (Longaretti & Toe 2017). The terms imply that teachers of such institutions must face greater challenges in their work. Researchers often point out that low-status schools should be considered in a different framework than schools with children of average status. We also believe that teachers of disadvantaged schools form a distinct group within the teacher community due to their work environment and the extraordinary methods they need to employ, therefore they require special training and professional help. The need for special training arises from multiple factors. First, teachers often face a broader set of tasks in low

SES schools (e.g., they have to teach pupils how to wash their hands, they must teach children who are much older than the average, and they might need to skip chapters). Second, the cultural divide between a middle-class teacher and pupils from a different financial and intellectual (often even ethnic) background might be so great that it becomes too difficult to establish the necessary environment for studying (Sleeter 2008; Nagy 2002). At the same time, pupils' low aspirations, limited knowledge, missing parental motivation, lack of support to study at home all make pedagogical tasks difficult.

Recently graduated teachers often encounter the most serious problem through the fact that they are unable to put their theoretical knowledge into practice, as teacher education is not aligned with the need of future practitioners. This phenomenon is amplified if recent graduates face children who come from a fundamentally different social background than those whom they had encountered during their teaching practice. In Hungary, teacher education institutions generally maintain special schools of teaching practice, where teacher education students spend the first part of their practice period. These schools admit that well-socialized children of high status, who are relatively well disciplined, require different pedagogical methods than average pupils.

Many countries attempt to resolve this contradiction. It is possible to involve professionals into teacher education who have significant experience in the matter. Thus, teacher education students can receive a first-hand practical account of school environments and potential methods to be employed with different student compositions (Hempel-Jorgensen et al. 2018; Longaretti & Toe 2017, Nagy 2009).

At the end of our study, we explore the possibilities of educating disadvantaged students in present-day Hungary. Teacher education is offered at 39 faculties of 23 higher education institutions, yet the special knowledge of educating disadvantaged children is not included in the system-wide curriculum. Nevertheless, some institutions have already sought to overcome this shortcoming. In the following, we provide an outline of some best practices at major teacher education institutions. Since Hungarian universities, with the notable exception of the University of

Miskolc, have not included early attempts in their curricula, we base our analysis on syllabi provided by university professors.

The University of Miskolc does not have a special school of teaching practice. The university operates in the most underprivileged county in Hungary. Most of its students come from the same county and begin to teach there upon graduation in schools with a high proportion of disadvantaged children. Therefore, teaching practice takes place at institutions with a high proportion of underprivileged and Roma children, which prepares teacher education students to future challenges from the start.

At the University of Szeged, a voluntary experimental program has been launched to prepare teacher education students for disadvantaged children's integrated education. Participating students become underprivileged children's mentors, which allow them to grasp the various problems caused by a disadvantaged background. Studying together provides an excellent opportunity to experiment with different methods. However, participants cannot gain classroom experience during the program.

At Eötvös Loránd University, there have been attempts to include teaching practice towards disadvantaged children into the curriculum. Teacher education students must visit institutions with a high proportion of low-status children. Sensitization programs, when professionals in the field talk about their work, are organized regularly. During community practice, connecting to disadvantaged children is encouraged.

At the University of Debrecen, it is not part of the curriculum to teach in a low SES school. Besides compulsory courses, teacher education students who wish to work in disadvantaged schools may choose to participate in the voluntary program which connects them to these institutions and prepares them to face the environment there.

Conclusion

In our study, we have attempted to provide a comprehensive overview of the system of Hungarian teacher education. Instead of exploring a specific phenomenon in detail, we have decided to underline the issues which contain the major characteristics and challenges of today. These points have been the following: changes in the system of teacher education, the path towards denominational variety, and the possibilities of disadvantaged children's education. The proportion of underprivileged children in Hungary is on the rise, while the structure of society has become more closed since the fall of communism. The social framework outlined in the first part of our study also reinforces this.

Teacher education in Hungary displays problems, challenges and characteristics which can be interpreted through the findings of the international literature (e.g., the implementation of the Bologna Process and its effects), although specific elements also emerge from the history, tradition and present social structures of the country. In our study, we have aimed at an exhaustive synthesis of these two threads, which, as we hope, offers invaluable insight into Hungarian teacher education.

References

Bacskai, K. (2015). *Iskolák a társadalom peremén.* [*Schools at the fringe of society*] Szeged: Belvedere Meridionale.

Bacskai, K., and Pusztai, G. (2015). Parochial Schools and PISA Effectiveness in Three Central European Countries. *Acta Universitatis Sapientiae Social Analysis,* 5 (II): 145-161.

Bocsi, V., Morvai, L. and Csokai, A. (2015). An Analysis of Teacher Education Students' Child-Rearing Values in a Cross-Border Area. In. *Challenges of Teacher Education in the Carpathian Basin,* edited by Pusztai G. and Ceglédi T. 117-128. Nagyvárad: Új Mandátum.

Brezsnyánszky, L. (2006). *A maga vájta meder. Gondolatok a formálódó tanárképzésről.* [*A self-created riverbed. Thoughts on teacher education in transformation*] Budapest: Gondolat.

Brezsnyánszky, L. and Fenyő, I. (eds.) 2009. *Gyakorlógimnázium a Simonyi úton.* [*A secondary school for teaching practice on Simonyi way*] Debrecen: KLTE /Acta Paedagogica Debrecina, 104.

Burnett, B. and Lampert, J. (2011). Teacher education and the Targeting of Disadvantage. *Creative Education,* 2 (V): 446–451.

Csapó, B. and Molnár, Gy. and Kinyó, L. (2009). A magyar oktatási rendszer szelektivitása a nemzetközi összehasonlító vizsgálatok eredményeinek tükrében [The selectivity of the Hungarian education system from the perspective of international comparative studies], *Iskolakultúra* 19 (III-IV): 3-13.

Castro, A. J., Kelly, J. and Shih, M. (2010). Resilience strategies for new teachers in high-needs areas. *Teaching and Teacher Education*, 26 (III): 622–629.

Coleman, J. S. et al. (1966). *Equality of Educational Opportunity.* Government Washington D. C.: Printing Office.

Csepeli, Gy. (2016). A Z nemzedék lehetséges életpályái. [Possible life paths of the Z generation] *Educatio,* 24 (IV): 509-515.

Darling-Hammond, L. (2010). Teacher education and the American future. *Journal of Teacher Education,* 61(I-II): 35-47.

Eurofound. 2017. *Social mobility in the EU.* Luxembourg: Publications Office of the European Union.

Eurostat. 2018. *Gini coefficient of equivalised disposable income. Last modified* November 6. http://appsso.eurostat.ec.europa.eu/nui/show.do?dataset=ilc_di12.

Hempel-Jorgensen, A., Cremin, T., Harris, D. and Chamberlain, L. (2018). "Pedagogy for Reading for Pleasure in Low Socio-Economic Primary Schools: Beyond 'Pedagogy of Poverty'"? *Literacy,* 52 (II): 86-94

Híves, T. and Kozma, T. (2014). Az expanzió vége? [The end of expansion?] *Educatio,* 22 (II): 239-252.

Hrubos, I. (2002). *A "bolognai folyamat." Európai trendek. A Bolognai Nyilatkozatból adódó strukturális változtatások megvalósíthatósága a magyar felsőoktatásban.* [*The Bologna Process. European trends. The changes laid out in the Bologna Declaration and their structural applicability in the Hungarian higher education*] Budapest: Oktatáskutató Intézet.

Hunyady, Gy. (2010a). Bologna és tanárképzés. [Bologna and Teacher Education.] *Felsőoktatási Szemle,* 4 (II): 101-106.

Hunyady, Gy. (ed.) (2010b). *Pedagógusképzés a „magyar bolognai rendszerben." A Nemzeti Bologna Bizottság Pedagógusképzési Albizottságának válogatott dokumentumai 2003-2010.* [*Teacher education in the "Hungarian Bologna system." Documents from the National Bologna Committee Teacher Education Subcommittee 2003-2010*] Budapest: ELTE Eötvös Kiadó.

Kozma, T. and Rébay, M. (eds.) (2008). *A bolognai folyamat Közép-Európában.* [*Bologna Process in Central Europe*] Budapest: Új Mandátum.

Lannert, J. (2010). A magyar pedagógusok munkaterhelése. [Hungarian teachers' workload] In *Társadalmi Riport 2010,* edited by Kolosi T. and Tóth I. Gy. 451-471. Budapest: TÁRKI.

Longaretti, L. and Toe, D. (2017). School Leaders' Perspectives on Educating Teachers to Work in Vulnerable Communities: New Insights from the Coal Face *Australian Journal of Teacher Education,* 42 (IV): 1-18.

Nagy, M. (2002). Cigány tanulók az iskolában. A tanárok beszélnek. [Roma pupils in school. Teacher accounts] *Magyar Pedagógia,* 102 (III): 301–331.

Nagy, M. (2004). Pályakezdés mint a pedagógusképzés középső fázisa. [Labor market entry as the middle stage of teacher education] *Educatio,* 13 (III): 375–390.

Nagy, M. (2009). Tanári kompetenciák és hátrányos helyzetű tanulók nevelése [Teacher competencies and the disfvantaged students' education] In. *A közoktatás méltányossági problémái és a tanárképzés.* [*Issues of fairness in public education and teacher education*] edited by Nagy, M.. 59-84. Eger: EKF.

Papp, Z. A. (2011). A roma tanulók aránya Magyarországon és a tanulói teljesítmények az általános iskolában. [The proportion of Roma pupils in Hungary and pupils' efficiency in primary school] In. *Asszimiláció, integráció, szegregáció* [*Assimilation, intagration, segregation*], edited by Bárdi, N. and Tóth, Á. 227-264. Budapest: MTA Kisebbségkutató Intézet.

Pócsik, O. 2015. *Pedagógusdinasztiák létjogosultsága pedagógus karrierpályák tükrében Magyarországon.* [*Teacher dynasties from the perspective of teacher career paths in Hungary*] *Iskolakultúra,* 25 (VII-VIII): 102-112.

Pukánszky, B. (2014). *A tanárképzés paradigmái és szerkezeti-tartalmi változásai Magyarországon.* [*Paradigms and structural-curricular changes of teacher education*] http://www.pukanszky.hu/postbologna.pdf.

Pusztai, G. (2006). Community and Social Capital in Hungarian Denominational Schools Today. *Religion and Society in Central and Eastern Europe,* 1 (I): 1-15.

Pusztai, G. (2010). Church Related Higher Education in Eastern and Central Europe In. *Art of life: Origins, Foundations and Perspectives,* edited by Juhant J. and Žalec B. 283-292. Münster: LIT Verlag.

Pusztai, G. (2015). *Pathways to success in higher education: Rethinking the Social Capital Theory in the Light of Institutional Diversity.* Frankfurt am Main: Peter Lang Verlag.

Pusztai, G. and Kovács, K. (eds.) (2015). *Ki eredményes a felsőoktatásban?* [*Who is efficient in higher education?*] Nagyvárad – Budapest: Partium – PPS – Új Mandátum.

Rice, S. (2008). Getting good teachers into challenging schools. *Curriculum Leadership,* 6 (XIV): 1–3.

Rónay, Z. (2018). Bologna húsz éve. [Twenty years of the Bologna Process] In. *A Borszem Jankótól Bolognáig. Neveléstudományi Tanulmányok,* edited by Fehérvári A. 165-186. Budapest: L'Harmattan. [*Borszem from Janko to Bologna. Educational Studies*]

Schanda, B. (2004). Staatskirchenrechtliche Kontexte der Theologischen Fakultäten in Ungarn. In. *Theologische Fakultäten an europäischen Universitäten. Rechtliche Situation und theologische Perspektiven,* edited by Loretan, A. 145-153. Münster: LIT Verlag. [State church contexts of the theological faculties in Hungary. In. *Theological faculties at European universities. Legal situation and theological perspectives*]

Staatskirchenrechtliche Kontexte der Theologischen Fakultäten in Ungarn. 2002. Bulletin ET. *Zeitschrift für Theologie in Europa,* 13 (II): 79-86. [State church contexts of the theological faculties in Hungary. 2002. Bulletin ET. *Journal of Theology in Europe*]

Sáska, G. (2015). Az elmúlt két évtized pedagógusképzési reformküzdelmei, kreditekben elbeszélve. [Reform processes in teacher education in the last two decades, told in credits] *Magyar Tudomány,* 176 (VII): 819-827.

Sleeter, Ch. E. (2008). Preparing white teachers for diverse students. In. *Handbook of research on teacher education: Enduring questions in changing contexts.* edited by Cochran-Smith, M., Feiman-Nemser, S. and and McIntyre D. J., 559-582. New York: Routledge, Taylor & Francis Group.

Soósné Faragó, M. (2010). A tanárképzés új (bolognai) rendszerének bemutatása. [Overview of the new (Bologna) structure of teacher education] *Új Pedagógiai Szemle,* 60 (III-IV) :50-68.

Szabó, L. T. (1998). *Tanárképzés Európában.* [*Teacher education in Europe*] Budapest: Oktatáskutató Intézet.

Szemerszki, M. (2015). A tanulói eredményesség dimenziói és háttértényezői [Dimensions and background factors of student efficiency], In. *Eredményesség az oktatásban,* [*Efficiency in education*] edited by Szemerszki, M. 52-91. Budapest: Oktatáskutató és Fejlesztő Intézet.

Szolár, É. (2010). A felsőoktatás reformja és a Bologna-folyamat Magyarországon. [Higher education reform and the Bologna Process in Hungary] *Magyar Pedagógia,* 110 (III): 239-263.

Unicef. 2012. *A gyermekszegénység mérése.* [*Measuring child poverty*] https://unicef.hu/wp-content/uploads/2014/11/unicef_RC10_magyar_sum-1.pdf.

Veroszta, Zs. (2015). Pályakép és szelekció a pedagóguspálya választásában. [Career outlook and selection in the choice of the teaching profession] *Educatio,* 25 (1): 47-62.

Veroszta, Zs. (2016). *Frissdiplomások 2015. Zárótanulmány.* [*Recent graduates 2015. Final study*] https://www.felvi.hu/pub_bin/dload/DPR_tanulmanyok/frissdiplomasok_zarotanulmany_2015.pdf.

In: An In Depth Look at Hungary
Editor: Esperanta Rompa
ISBN: 978-1-53615-351-4

Chapter 3

PROTECTION OF THE BOHEMIAN CROWN'S EASTERN BORDER WITHIN THE KINGDOM OF HUNGARY: THE FORM AND STRUCTURE OF UNITS DEPLOYED IN BORDER PROTECTION IN THE EARLY MODERN PERIOD

Martin Krůl and Jan Saheb*
The Centre for Economic and Social History,
University of Ostrava, Ostrava, Czech Republic

ABSTRACT

Border protection received increased attention in early modern times; particularly the mountain ranges, which served as a natural defensive zone when entering the country, becoming the target for fortification activities and the concentration spot for the military units designed to defend them.

* Corresponding Author's Email: jan.saheb@centrum.cz.

The eastern border of the Bohemian crownlands with the Kingdom of Hungary was also the border between Hungary and Moravia and Hungary and Silesia. This became evident especially in the 16th century in the structure of the units designed for border protection. Warfare in the turbulent Hungarian times, the advancement of the Ottoman Army, and the continuing threat of the Hungarian anti-Habsburg uprising, which lasted throughout the 17th century, represented a permanent danger. The border with Hungary was therefore a place whose defence attracted the attention of estate representatives and later also the highest military bodies of Moravia and Silesia. The forms of military and paramilitary units represented a complex organizational structure; the defence of the country was secured by both the state (royal) and the provincial (estate) units, as well as the paramilitary units of the subjects (inhabitants) living in the border areas. This development reflected qualitative changes in the military sector, and the far-reaching consequences of the process also had a societal impact. The process can be concisely summarised within the historiographical concept of 'military revolution'. The present contribution follows the above-mentioned issues primarily through investigating the development of irregular armed forces formed of local citizens, which were deployed in border protection.

Keywords: The Kingdom of Hungary, Moravia, Silesia, borders, the early modern period, military history, fortification

INTRODUCTION

In the early modern period, threat of war influenced virtually all areas of the society. Although the Bohemian crownlands were not burdened by war events to such an extent as, for example, the Empire or Hungary, areas with increased threat of military activities could still be found. Those included the eastern border of the country, which at the same time formed the border between two Crown lands, Moravia and Silesia, and the Kingdom of Hungary. Turkish presence imperilled the southeast border of the Habsburg monarchy for most of the 16th century and in the period after the Thirty Years' War, when its expansive policy once again focused on penetrating Europe. However, it was not only the Turkish troops that worried the Moravian and Silesian borders in the given period; the units of the anti-Habsburg Hungarian rebels also represented a source of danger. In the 17th and early 18th centuries, they repeatedly allied with the Ottoman Empire, and their expansive efforts resulted in the second siege of Vienna in 1683, after which the Ottoman Empire was gradually forced out of the area.

The defence systems of the eastern border with Hungary thus faced a military threat in the long run, practically from the first half of the 16th to the first third of the 18th century. As a result, they stood in the centre of attention of estate representatives and later also the highest military bodies of Moravia and Silesia. The paper focuses on small field fortifications, a form of defence of the access corridors in mountain areas. Fortifications, of course, could not fulfil their function without the presence of a human factor, and different types of units were deployed in border protection; the defence of the country was secured by state (royal) and provincial (estate) units, as well as paramilitary units composed of subjects (inhabitants) living in the border areas, and the forms of such military and paramilitary units represented a complex organizational structure. The units formed of local citizens, which are the main interest of the present paper, proved largely successful and remained in existence until the beginning of the 19th century. Here, the aim is not to study the circumstances, the course and the consequences of the individual military engagements, or the Hungarian military invasions, but to analyse the activation mechanisms, forms and jurisdictional branches of the individual defence components on the Moravia-Silesian-Hungarian border, as their development reflected qualitative changes in the military sector, and the process had far-reaching consequences for the society as a whole. This has been concisely summarised within the Western European and American historiographical concept of 'military revolution' [1].

Border Protection and the Construction of Frontier Fortifications

It was at the site of the Ottoman province and the Hungarian territory where a military cordon formed, stretching from the Slavonic-Croatian border to Transylvania. After the Battle of Mohács (29 August 1526), its structure gradually evolved and was adapted in view of the long-standing Turkish military presence. In 1577, the defence of the military borders was centralized in terms of its division into separate sections, securing financing and unity of command. The constant presence of military troops in the forts and their long-term service made them permanent crews. At the same time, due to their location in the fortress buildings, they can be seen as quasi-barrack compounds, serving the purposes of mobility and accommodation of troops during summer and winter quarters. The backbone of the entire military frontier was in the main, large fortresses with troops of about 1,000 to 1,500 men, further supported by medium-sized fortresses comprising about 500 soldiers. This structure was complemented by several smaller castles with crews of approximately two hundred people, and a large number of small guard and log cabins [2].

In addition to the main military cordon, these fortresses were also built, though to a much lesser extent, at the borders of the historical provinces neighbouring Hungary. The borders of Moravia and Silesia with Hungary were formed by the Western Carpathians, which represented a natural obstacle. Moravia was closer to the places of war or armed conflict outbreak, and due to its longer borderline and greater permeability of mountain regions was much more vulnerable than Silesia. On the other hand, the only direct border contact between Silesia and Hungary was just 49 kilometres long. The possibilities for active border defence were secured by the fact that the only crossing suitable for transfer of larger units was the Jablunkov Pass. This is also where the land route representing the most important connection between Silesia and Hungary was situated. In view of the dangers of military and marauding incursions, fortification activities were taking place in the aforementioned border regions of Moravia and Silesia from the 1520s. Initially, it was defence in the form of so-called "indentions" (i.e., deliberate destruction of border forest areas designed to make them less permeable), designed to slow down the enemy's attack. It was only later that a system of field fortifications was built in the area of the Moravian-Silesian-Hungarian border, especially in the passes, which, together with the original border castles, played a key role in border defence during the 16th and 17th centuries.

Until the middle of the 17th century, these fortification activities reflected the estate-sovereign dualism. During the 16th century, the maintenance of fortifications fell among the competencies of individual estates, which approved the protection of access corridors at the borders of the country at their sessions (diets). In the narrow sense, the implementation of these measures stood on the individual noblemen, that is, vassals of the Czech kings (i.e., the bishops of Olomouc in Moravia, and the dukes of Těšín in Silesia). In the Duchy of Těšín, the situation changed after 1653, when the local Piast branch died out and the duchy became a part of the ruling Habsburgs' chamber property [3]. The regulations concerning mountain crossings and their indention generally responded to the increased activity of Ottoman troops operating in Hungary; individual regulations of the Moravian and Silesian land diets regarding the indention of border forests have been found dated as early as 1620s. However, the extent to which they were, in fact, implemented is disputable, as there are no other written records of their existence on the Moravian-Silesian-Hungarian border.

As for the construction of fortifications on the Moravian-Silesian-Hungarian border, one of the earliest sources of evidence is the retrospective reports of two Silesian chroniclers of the 17th century, Jacob Schickfuss and Frideric Luca. Both of them state that the construction of the fortifications guarding the land route in the Jablunkov Pass did not take place until 1574 [4]. It was probably connected with the defence against the impending attack of the troops of Sigismund Báthory, Prince of Transylvania and the brother of the newly elected Polish King Stephen Báthory (unsuccessfully opposed by Maximilian III of Austria) [5].

The number of small fortifications on the Silesian-Moravian-Hungarian border was significantly extended during the turbulent times of the Thirty Years' War (1618–1648). At the same time, the settlement process in the Beskydy Mountains and the White Carpathians culminated and stabilized, which played an important role in the creation and localization of individual land fortifications (so-called *šance[s]*). Their location was related to the colonization coming from the Hungarian border. The economic activity of new settlers (especially the Wallachians) resulted in significant deforestation and the emergence of new trails in the border area, thereby reducing its natural defensive capacity. Detailed reports about the construction of individual border fortifications come from the first half of the 17th century, the most important of which were the so-called Jablunkov land fortifications (*šances*). This fortification system defended the whole northern section of the Silesian-Moravian-Hungarian border and belonged to the strategically significant supporting points of land defence [6].

The significance of the Jablunkov Pass in terms of its position allowed for its strategic serving as the only direct link between Silesia and Hungary. Let us now briefly comment on the genesis of this fortification system. During the 16th and the beginning of the 17th century, the defence of the Jablunkov Pass consisted mainly in the construction of field *šances*, most often in the shape of square redoubts or star forts. The exception was the central point, the Grand (Jablunkovská) Šance in the form of a baroque bastion fortification gradually supplemented with other fortification elements such as the hornwork, surrounded by other outworks. Three larger fortifications with a more complicated typology – the Great Šance (fort with bastions), the Small Šance (star fort) and the Old Šance (redoubt with half-bastions), formed the main points of defence followed by the Volská Šance in the form of a bigger redoubt on the Polish border. Among these fortifications, a system of smaller redoubts was built to serve as a communicative or forward fortification [7]. On the Silesian-Hungarian border, a system of fortifications referred to as Jablunkovské Šance [Jablunkov Forts] was gradually built during the period under review, and during the course of its existence it prevented enemy troops from entering the country several times, demonstrating its importance in the border protection system. Although the condition of these mostly field elements combined with wooden components was subject to deterioration several years after their construction and they often had to be repaired, they protected the mountain crossing efficiently, unlike the unprotected Moravia, which was attacked several times during the period and many of its towns and villages were plundered. That is why an order was issued to build field fortifications on the Moravian-Hungarian border, mostly in the form of simple redoubts.

The construction of several fortifications effectively prevented the direct hostile invasions of the Hungarian insurgents in 1605, 1621, 1645, 1678, 1680, 1688, and 1704. The significance of the Jablunkov Forts is also evidenced by the fact that, after the penetration through the unprotected pass at the Polish town of Živec, violent action was taken by the Kuruc insurgents in Silesia, which affected the city of Bílsko and the North Moravian dominion of Hukvaldy [8]. Military operations at the Jablunkov Forts did not have the form of large military manoeuvres involving massive armies. The crews were made up of military units ranging in size from 50 to 300 men, or troops from the Silesian "hueste" (Ger. *das Landesaufgebot*, i.e., mostly non-professional groups of armed men drawn from broader public) and recruits who supplemented them [9]. The significance of the fortifications was already well understood by the important military theorist and Habsburg General Raimondo Montecuccoli, who in 1648 suggested that the fortifications in the Habsburg territory representing the "key to Hungary" be maintained and modernized, and occupied by a permanent crew of 200 men [10].

Das Landesaufgebot

During the period of 16th to 18th century, the Moravian-Silesian-Hungarian border protection was one of the major interests of the Moravian and Silesian estate authorities as well as the relevant components of the state bureaucratic apparatus. It can be said that the organization of defence in the area showed partial disproportions between and within the two countries (Moravia and Silesia). Substantial power in the organisation of defence in both countries was maintained by the Land Diet (Landtag), which was in charge of approving the amount of revenue for army maintenance, but also calling for the so-called Landesaufgebot. The executive power in defence organisation in Moravia was in the hands of the provincial and individual regional governors; in Silesia, it was the *Königliche Oberambt* in Wrocław or the heads of individual principalities. The supreme body in the structure concerning military and defence affairs was the The Aulic War Council in Vienna.

The obligation to build military contingents applied to all the countries of the monarchy and was bound to the approval of individual countries, whose shares were determined on the basis of financial estimates. A new form of recruitment of military forces was the hiring of wage soldiers and troops, who had to be approved by the estates. The ruler turned to the estates in the matters of building troops in two ways; in the first case, which predominated in the initial period, he required the delivery and maintenance of a certain number and type of troops, including weaponry and equipment. Gradually, from the time of Maximilian I (1493–1519), this was replaced with the sovereign's demands on the estates for the provision of the relevant fees for which the army was recruited, armed and remunerated. This financial quota required in connection with the Turkish threat after the Battle of Mohács, which was called the Turkish tax (Türckensteuer), gradually acquired the character of a permanent fee [11].

The other component of the country's defence was the Landesaufgebot. This component can be described as a tactic which had survived from the medieval period and depended solely on the will of the individual estates of the country. These "ad hoc" armed troops were built essentially in two ways, but each time depending on the provisions of the Land Diet. Either the country had to set up a number of cavalrymen and infantrymen with wagons and rifles, or it was the duty of the individual authorities to take over this responsibility. As a rule, the estates committed to a number of foot soldiers and horsemen on the basis of the estimated value of their land assets or to arm every 20th, 10th, sometimes 5th, of their subjects (citizens owning property). In Silesia, for example, there was an obligation to put on duty one rider from each property worth more than 3,000 guldens. The unrecruited subjects were obliged to provide for the cost of food for those who had been recruited for the Landesaufgebot. For these purposes, an inventory of the population, especially for towns and villages, was drawn up and transmitted to the Chief Governor (Landeshauptmann). He then drafted every fifth, tenth, fifteenth or twentieth man as needed. Indeed, the real ability of the Landesaufgebot made up of armed subjects (not professional soldiers) and its combat morale was, of course, questionable. Not only did the subjects often appear for enlistment (the so-called "mustruňk") with considerable delay, but the combat ability of these units was reduced by a high rate of desertion. Thus, in Moravia and Silesia, this inefficient way of defending the country was virtually abandoned after 1605, when the Landesaufgebot failed to protect the country from the invasion of the Hungarian troops led by Stephen Bocskai [12]. The devastation of border areas demonstrated an urgent need to respond to the development of European warfare. The arrival of professional military units, their targeted training, and the application of new technological advances influencing tactics and combat strategy, put the existing system of summoning the Landesaufgebot completely out of date. The questions of the inevitable transformation of the territory defence system were dealt with in 1615 at the General Assembly of the Bohemian crownlands (Generallandtag). The result was a measure which can be seen as a precursor of the idea of a permanent army; the Landesaufgebot was to be replaced by the obligation for each country to pay a small staff of colonels, whose duty was to hire a specified number of soldiers in the event of acute danger to the territory. In practice, before the outbreak of the Thirty Years' War, this system was first implemented in Moravia, with Albrecht von Wallenstein being one of the three permanent Moravian colonels [13].

Before the Thirty Years' War, there were also fundamental changes in the ways of protection of the Moravian-Silesian-Hungarian border, because the existing practice had proven retrograde and completely unsatisfactory. During the Thirty Years' War (1618–1648), the forts (the *šances*) on the Moravian-Silesian-Hungarian border were already occupied by permanent professional crews, and from the middle of the 17th century by troops of the imperial army.

The Journey towards a Standing Army

In the 16th and 17th centuries, two main principles of building troops were applied in Europe, which were related to the traditional dualist division of power between the estates and the sovereign. Since the Landesaufgebot had shown to be anachronistic already during the second half of the 16th century, modernization of border defence systems was inevitable. Both the estates and the sovereign gradually opted for the recruitment of professional soldiers [14]. The obligation to build military contingents applied to all the countries of the monarchy and was bound to the approval of individual countries, whose shares were determined on the basis of financial estimates. The problem was, however, that these troops were not to be deployed beyond the borders of the given country. While the estates of each country were limited to the recruitment of these regiments (there was a "numerus clausus"), the sovereign was only limited by accessible funds. Most of the mercenary regiments were thus subordinated to him and central military councils (the monarch issued the so-called colonel patents to the individual condottiers). A turning point in the military development was the Thirty Years' War; while at the beginning of the conflict the habits of the Middle Ages (whether in tactics, strategy, funding, ways of building troops, securing supplies and accommodation) prevailed, then, after its end, the army represented a completely different apparatus.

A major change, foreshadowing the arrival of modern absolutist states in Europe, was the establishment of standing armies. Their long-term provision (including accommodation) required changes in the organization of tax collection and the associated centralization and bureaucratization of state administration, which necessarily had to be reflected in the civilian population. Common practice prior to the outbreak of the Thirty Years' War was the hiring of troops only for the duration of the conflict, after which the soldiers would be dismissed [15]. However, this model proved unfavourable in long-term war campaigns, for several reasons. New soldiers had to be recruited and again subjected to training, which was inefficient in terms of time and finances. After their dismissal, the investments were lost, and a model of long-term service throughout the year began to be promoted. The specific feature of the Thirty Years' War was the military-business system, perfected by, for example, the personalities of Albrecht of Wallenstein [16]. Technical innovation and the improvement of tactical formations required regular training of soldiers as well as weapons handling. After the temporary predominance of mercenary units, keeping military crews even in peacetime proved to be most efficient. Although the maintenance of the permanent "winter war people" was common even during the Fifteen Years' War in Hungary (1593–1606), the real origin of the Habsburg army is considered to be only in 1649, when Emperor Ferdinand III issued a resolution that 4,000 cavalrymen and 10,000 members of the infantry be maintained even during peacetime [17]. The consequences of the establishment of a standing army and its professionalization were naturally reflected in the Silesian-Moravian-Hungarian border area defence system. During the 1660s, the existing fortification systems (especially in the Jablunkov Pass) were transformed into the seats of permanent garrison and occupied by a fixed number of men throughout the year. In the case of acute danger, auxiliary units of border guards from the episcopal militia, composed of the local citizens, were sent to the border.

THE EPISCOPAL MILITIA BORDER PATROL

In the period of 16th – 18th centuries, two specific bodies emerged as parts of the Moravian-Silesian-Hungarian border defence system – the so-called *portáš[es]* (Ger. *Portaschen*) and *vybranec[s]* (from the Czech "*vybrat*" – "choose, select"), civilian border patrol groups of the Olomouc episcopal militia, having a transitional character between the system of the Landesaufgebot and standing army units. These groups were initially called "ad hoc" only in the event of an acute threat to the border, but later developed into permanent auxiliary corps of the regular army, whose mission was to guard the border. Let us now focus more closely on the genesis of these groups.

The specifics of the Moravian military organization include the Olomouc bishops' jurisdiction over their own militia, and the *portáš* groups, who were initially immediately subordinated to the sovereign, and later to the Moravian estates. In the Silesian border defence system, the jurisdiction was retained by the Duchy of Těšín Diet, which was undoubtedly related both to the complexity of administrative relations in Silesia and Těšín's geographical location on the very border with Hungary, Poland, and

Moravia. Besides the episcopal militia, there was also a parallel to the Moravian portáš groups – the *vybranec* groups, which were subject to the jurisdiction of the Land Military Command in this principality [18]. The defence system in Moravia and Silesia was thus very complex in terms of ruling powers, including the estates as well as the provincial authorities, the Olomouc bishop, and the sovereign, which greatly reduced combat readiness and cooperation among the various defence branches. Although there had been efforts on the part of the Aulic War Council to unify the command of all the contingents since the 1680s, the episcopal militia, the portášes and the vybranecs continued to maintain their autonomy vis-à-vis the central command [19].

***

Let us first focus on the issue of the Olomouc episcopal militia (*Bisthumbs-landts Musquetier und Dragonern*) and the status of the so-called bishop Wallachian units (*Bisthumbs-Valachen*). Due to the very specific status of the Roman Catholic Archdiocese of Olomouc and its mensal and feudal property in the legal system of Moravia, the heads of the Catholic Church in Moravia had the right to convene and command their own militia, irrespective of the decisions of the provincial authorities and even the land military command [20]. The episcopal battalions included, besides the conscripts from the immediate episcopal mensal and feudal property, soldiers recruited from individual manors, chapels, and monasteries.

The principle of summoning the episcopal militia can be compared, in analogy, with the summoning of the Landesaufgebot (in which the Olomouc Archdiocese did not participate). The basis was the recruiting of the subjects, governed in the 17th century by the data in the internal conscriptions of the Olomouc diocese property. The point of assembly of the episcopal militia was Kroměříž, where both foot soldiers and cavalry members had to meet, usually within a week or two from the dispatch of the relevant patents. A specific place within the episcopal militia was occupied by the Wallachians, recruited exclusively from two estates, namely Kelč and Hukvaldy. In 1705, for example, the episcopal administration in the temporalibus called only the Wallachians who had been seated in the foothills of these lands, explaining that this was due to their excellent physical dispositions for military service and knowledge of the eastern Moravia border area, which they were supposed to protect. The ethnically non-Wallachian population of towns and villages of both estates were obliged to financially support the units of the Kelč and Hukvaldy Wallachians [21]. For example, in 1677 Karl II von Liechtenstein-Kastelkorn, the Prince-Bishop of Olomouc, called to arms, besides 37 dragoons and 117 musketeers, another 400 Wallachians only to secure the borders and passes in the Hukvaldy estate. In August 1682, there were 121 Wallachians employed on the border of the Hukvaldy estate with Hungary, and similarly during *the Rákóczi Uprising* in the first decade of the 18th century [22].

The episcopal militia's operational area was usually in land passes, near which the Landesaufgebot and later the land mercenary army concentrated. The Wallachians from the Hukvaldy and Kelč estates regularly guarded the border region of north-eastern Moravia adjacent to Hungary, with secondary centres of their operating space being individual episcopal forts. In connection with the activities of the episcopal militia in the years of acute threats to the country in the form of enemy incursions, it is also necessary to mention the co-operation of these units with an intelligence network of spies. Although they were outside the armed forces, their operations were essentially interwoven with the episcopal militia. Spies on the Hungarian side of the land border were usually Wallachians from the Moravian border regions. From the information sources available we know that many of them were recruited even from the subjects who were settled on the Hungarian side of the borderbut served in the service of Olomouc bishops [23].

***

Analogously to the episcopal militia, the so-called land portášes (Landesportatschen) were involved in the defence of the Moravian-Hungarian border from 1638. These were smaller guard troops comprised of the Wallachian population of the Moravian borderland estates in the Uherské

Hradiště and Přerov Regions, which did not belong to the Olomouc diocese, but to secular authorities. The competencies associated with the activity of the portáš corps were determined by the sovereign and his administration (the Moravian Regional Chief Governor, Ger. *Landeshauptmann von Mähren*). However, with the recurring need to activate the groups, this system proved to be less flexible as it could not adequately respond to current dangers. That is why Emperor Leopold I issued with his rescripts from 1666 and 1667 a permission to call the portáš corps to the Moravian Diet. However, the costs associated with it were borne by the Treasury, although Moravian estates were also temporarily involved [24]. A fundamental break in the portáš groups' further existence was the decision of the Moravian Diet from 1716, which decided to establish a corps of land portášes as a permanent security institution operating in the east of Moravia. The monarch agreed with the proposal and, with a rescript of 3 April 1717, ordered that the corps continue to be governed by the Moravian provincial administration and, consequently, financially supported at the expense of the Estate Treasury [25]. During the first half of the 18th century, there were attempts to professionalize the portáš corps; according to the imperial decree of December 1740, it was to accept only unmarried men, whose performance of the service would not be hindered by other jobs or providing for a family or homestead. At the turn of the 18th and 19th centuries, the jurisdiction of the portáš was temporarily extended to Silesia, but in 1827, with the approval of Emperor Francis I, the Silesian portášes were dissolved. In Moravia, the portáš corps ceased to exist in October 1830 [26].

***

The Silesian parallel of the episcopal militia and portáš corps operating in Moravia were the units of the so-called vybranecs, subject to the jurisdiction of the provincial military command of the Duchy of Těšín. Like the episcopal militia and the portáš corps, the vybranecs were recruited almost exclusively from local subjects. The beginnings of the recruitment of the Wallachians from the Duchy of Těšín mountain areas to defend the border mountain range are connected with the Thirty Years' War. At that time, they often replaced busy imperial troops, or supplemented them. Their number was based on the degree of danger to the territory, for example, in 1621, 150 Wallachians and subjects were sent to defend the Jablunkov Pass, in the years 1644 and 1645, the guard service was performed on the Silesian-Hungarian border by 400 Wallachians [27]. Although the defence of the Silesian-Hungarian border was to be secured by all Silesian principalities, it was mostly covered solely by the easternmost Duchy of Těšín, at its own expense. At the order of the Military Command or the Central Silesian authorities (the Silesian Landeshauptmann and later the High Authority), Elizabeth Lucretia, the Duchess of Těšín (1599–1653) ordered calling the Landesaufgebot composed of the subjects living in the territory. In addition, local subjects contributed to the construction of the fortifications in the Jablunkov Pass (the so-called šances) [28].

The vybranecs remained significant even after the end of the Thirty Years' War, as they were regularly deployed and became an important part of the Silesian border defence. Most of the information on their activities has been preserved since the period of both Hungarian anti-Habsburg uprisings in the last third of the 17th and early 18th centuries. Their numbers in this period ranged from a few dozen to hundreds of men. The influence of the vybranecs (back then they were referred to as *Land-Vybranzen* or *Landleuten*, which reflected their integration into the Silesian structures) is documented for decades after the conclusion of the Treaty of Szatmár in 1711. When the Great Fort was occupied by the Prussian troops on 8 February 1741 during the First Silesian War, it was defended by 120 men together with the Wallis regiment of 104 men under the command of Lieutenant Colonel Johann O'Reilly [29]. Until the end of the 18th century, the vybranec formations were gradually disappearing, as evidenced by the fact that two corps of Moravian portášes were deployed to maintain order in the southern mountainous part of the Duchy of Těšín from the end of the 18th century [30].

From the middle of the 17th century, the vybranecs were organised on a military basis in troops of 100 to 200 men, headed by the commander, officers, and primaplanas, and often had Těšín noblemen as their leaders (such as Jan Jindřich Šimonský, Jan Daniel Spens Boden, Václav

Tschammer or Václav Rostek of Bzí). Also, the composition of the troops was no longer a purely domestic affair, as the individual soldiers came not only from Wallachia, but also from the wider territory of Těšín Silesia, Poland, Bohemia, and even Sweden [31].

The main governing bodies were the *Königliche Oberambt* in Wrocław and the *Königliche Teschnische Ambt* in Těšín. It was their responsibility to recruit new men who had to take an oath, be enlisted and immediately put in service. The service was long-lasting; the vybranecs served usually 15, but in some cases up to 50 years. The operational area consisted of a wide mountain area from the Polish to the Moravian border, with the greatest attention being paid to the Silesian-Hungarian border on the southern slopes of the Beskydy Mountains. A significant defensive element here was the system of fortifications with the main fortress in Mosty u Jablunkova, supplemented by a number of other fortifications of different character [32].

The vybranec troops gradually evolved into regular units deployed in the Silesian border defence. Originally these were the troops recruited from the Wallachian subjects, which may be considered as a form of the Landesaufgebot; following the change in the legal status of the Duchy of Těšín after the death of the last Piast, Elizabeth Lucretia of Těšín, in 1653, they were shifted into the Silesian regular armed services (here they are mentioned besides the land militias and referred to as land vybranecs) and no longer governed by the estates, but by the central authorities (namely the Königliche Oberambt in Wrocław) [33].

CONCLUSION

What can be summed up in the conclusion on the issue of the Moravian-Silesian-Hungarian border protection and the forms and structure of the military units operating during the early modern period? It can be said that until the beginning of the 16th century border defence rested almost exclusively on state decisions. Although the Landesaufgebot and its combat ability represented a significant anachronism at the turn of the 17th century, a fundamental transformation of the country's defence system did not occur until shortly before the Thirty Years' War. The original system continued to be transformed in Moravia into the form of episcopal militia and portáš groups, called irregularly in the events of acute border threats, these units serving as mere auxiliary corps of the regular mercenary and later of the imperial armies, and their mission was to guard borders and passes. In Silesia, troops of the so-called vybranecs were established parallel to the episcopal and portáš groups. While until the beginning of the 18th century the episcopal militia was called "ad hoc" only in the case of a threat to the given section of the Moravian-Hungarian border, the units of portášes and the vybranecs became regular auxiliary guard components of the imperial army during the second half of the 17th and the 18th centuries. Service in military units and units of the episcopal militia also represented an important and sought-after source of income in the livelihood of the border guards and their families. Evidence is found not only in their long-term service but also in the requests for re-entry into service. Account may also be taken of the increase in the social status of the service members, which is evident mainly in connection with the Moravian portáš guards [34].

It was only during the advancing centralization and professionalization, which was significant of the modern army of the 18th century, that these two specific components gradually became ana-chronistic and were replaced by regular units. In a sense, this professionalization, gradually crystallizing from the second half of the 17th century, can be perceived in the wider context of the transformation of the military as a whole, in the context of the so-called military revolution. The gradual professionalization of the above-mentioned armed forces may serve as an example of the broad social impact of these changes on the economic and social conditions of early modern life in the Moravian-Silesian-Hungarian border area. The irregular armed units document the diversity of defensive structures in Moravia and Silesia and prove the complexity of military in the early modern age.

REFERENCES

[1] In the Czech scientific literature, the historiographical concept of military revolution has been summarised in Prchal, Vítězslav: *Společenstvo hrdinů. Válka a reprezentační strategie českomoravské aristokracie 1550–1750*. Praha 2015 [*Fellowship of Heroes. War and the Representative Strategies of the Bohemian-Moravian Aristocracy between 1550 and 1750*. Prague 2015], pp. 25–65.

[2] On military border see, for example, Pálffy, Géza: The Border Defense System in Hungary in the Sixteenth and Seventeenth Centuries. In: *A Millennium of Hungarian Military History. War and Society in East Central Europe*. Volume XXXVII. New York 2002, pp. 111–135; ibid.: *Türkenabwehr, Grenzsoldatentum und die militärisierung der Gesellschaft in Ungarn in der frühen Neuzeit*. Historisches Jahrbuch 123, 2003, pp. 111–148; Winkelbauer, Thomas: *Österreichische Geschichte 1522–1699. Teil 1: Ständefreiheit und Fürstenmacht*. Wien 2003, pp. 429–444. [Turkish defense, border soldiers and the militarization of society in Hungary in the early modern period. *Historical Yearbook* 123, 2003, pp. 111-148; Winkelbauer, Thomas: *Austrian History 1522-1699. Part 1: Freedom of the Order and Princely Power*.]

[3] Korbelářová, Irena – Žáček, Rudolf: *Těšínsko – země Koruny české*. [*Těšín Silesia – a Bohemian Crownland*]. Český Těšín, 2008, p. 137.

[4] Schickfuss, Jakob. New Vermehrete schlesische Chronica und Landes Beschreibung, III. Teil. Bresslau, 1624, pp. 239–240, Luca, Frideric: Schlesiens curieuse Denckwürdigkeiten, oder vollkommene Chronica von Ober- und Nieder- Schlesien. Franckfurt am Mayn 1689, p. 667. [*New Multiply Silesian Chronica and Landes Description*, III. Part. Bresslau, 1624, pp. 239-240, Luca, Frideric: *Silesian curieuse denunciations, or perfect Chronica of Upper and Lower Silesia*]

[5] Other border fortresses were also prepared to defend themselves against possible invasions, including the Hukvaldy Castle. See Saheb, Jan: Instrukce olomouckého biskupa Jana Mezouna z Telče z roku 1576 k zajištění obrany hradu Hukvaldy v případě války s Polsko-

litevskou unií. *Práce a studie Muzea Beskyd* 17 [The Order of the Olomouc Bishop Jan Mezoun from Telč from 1576 Concerning the Defence of the Hukvaldy Castle in the war with the Polish-Lithuanian Union. In: *Works and Studies of Museum Beskyd* 17, 2006], pp. 67–73.

[6] Krůl, Martin. Stav výzkumu novověkých opevnění slezsko-uhersko-polské hranice. In: *Polní opevnění od třicetileté války do roku 1945. Sborník Národního památkového ústavu, územního odborného* pracoviště vJosefově, 2010 [The state of research into the modern fortifications on the Silesian-Hungarian-Polish border. In: *Field Fortifications from the Thirty Years' War to 1945. Anthology of the National Heritage Institute*, Regional Office in Josefov 2010], pp. 6–18; ibid.: Fortyfikacje górskie Przełęczy Jabłonkowskiej. In: *Twierdza Srebrnogórska IV. Wojna Siedmioletnia w Sudetach i nowożytne fortyfikacje górskie. Wrocław*, 2013, pp. 59–74. [Mountain fortifications of the Jabłonkowska Pass. In: *Srebrna Góra Fortress IV. Seven-year war in the Sudetenland and modern mountain fortifications.*]

[7] Krůl, Martin; Nováková, Pavlína. *Jablunkovské šance*. Český Těšín 2005.

[8] Saheb, Jan. Kurucký vpád na hukvaldské panství roku 1680. *Těšínsko* 48 [The Kuruc Invasion in Hukvaldy in 1680. In: *Těšínsko* 48], 2005, č. 1, pp. 7–12, Vašutová, Lenka: Kurucký vpád na Moravu a města hukvaldského panství. In: *Kurucké vojny a ich odkaz v histórii, kultúre a umení* [The Kuruc Invasion in Moravia and towns of the Hukvaldy dominion. In: *The Kuruc Wars and their Legacy in History, Culture, and Art*]. Dolný Kubín–Český Těšín 2012, pp. 114–124; Pindur, David: Kurucký vpád do Bílska roku 1682 a jeho odraz v historiografii. In: Kurucké vojny a ich odkaz v histórii, kultúre a umení [The Kuruc Invasion in Bílsko in 1682 and its reflection in historiography. In: *The Kuruc Wars and their Legacy in History, Culture, and Art*]. Dolný Kubín–Český Těšín, 2012, pp. 125–142.

[9] Swieteczký, Bedřich. Kurucké války na Slovensku [The Kuruc Wars in Slovakia]. *Praha*, 1929, pp. 30–31.

[10] Veltzé, Alois von: Ausgewaehlte Schriften des Raimund Fürsten Montecuccoli General-Lieutenant und Feldmarschall, II. Band. Wien, 1899, p. 126, Dudík, Beda: Schweden in Böhmen und Mähren 1640–1650. Wien, 1879, p. 412. [*Selected writings of Raymond Prince Montecuccoli Lieutenant General and Field Marshal*, II. Volume. Vienna, 1899, p. 126, Dudík, *Beda: Sweden in Bohemia and Moravia*]

[11] Orzechowski, Kazimierz. *Historia ustroju Śląska 1202–1740*. Wrocław, 2005, pp. 151 –152; Maroń, Jerzy: *Wojna trzydziestoletnia na Śląsku. Aspekty militarne.* Wrocław–Racibórz, 2008, p. 38. [*The history of the system of Silesia 1202-1740.* Wrocław, 2005, pp. 151 - 152; Maroń, Jerzy: *Thirty Years' War in Silesia. Military aspects.*]

[12] Měšťánek, Tomáš. *Poměry na Moravě na přelomu 16. a 17. století v období válek tureckých a povstání Štěpána Bočkaje* [*Moravia at the Turn of the 16th and 17th centuries in the Time of the Turkish Wars and Stephen Bocskai's Uprising*]. Uherské Hradiště 1997, from p. 55 onwards; Saheb, Jan: Události patnáctileté války v Uhrách (1593–1608) ve světle korespondence olomouckých biskupů Stanislava Pavlovského a Františka z Ditrichštejna. In: *Mezi Martem a Memorií. Prameny osobní povahy k vojenským dějinám* 16.–19. století [The Events of the Fifteen Years' War in Hungary (1593 – 1608) in the Light of the Correspondence of the Olomouc Bishops Stanislav Pavlovsky and Franz von Dietrichstein. In: *Between Mart and Memoria. Sources of Personal Character in the Military History of 16th to 19th century*]. *Pardubice*, 2011, pp. 27–38.

[13] Petráň, Josef a kol. (ed.): Příběhy Jindřicha Hýzrla z Chodů [The Tales of Jindřich Hýrzle of Chody]. *Praha*, 1979, pp. 385–386.

[14] Winkelbauer, Thomas. *Österreichische Geschichte 1522–1699. Teil 1: Ständefreiheit und Fürstenmacht*. Wien, 2003, pp. 409–410. [*Austrian History 1522-1699. Part 1: Freedom of the Order and Princely Power.*]

[15] Mareš, Pavel. Organizace, výstroj a výzbroj vojska, financování a zásobování armád, způsoby boje. In: *Rytíři renesančních Čech ve válkách* [Army organization, equipment and armaments, financing and

supply of armies, ways of fighting. In: *Knights of Renaissance Bohemia in Wars*]. *Praha*, 2016, pp. 53–62.

[16] Winkelbauer, Thomas. *Österreichische Geschichte 1522–1699. Teil 1: Ständefreiheit und Fürstenmacht*. Wien, 2003, pp. 409–420. [*Austrian History 1522-1699. Part 1: Freedom of the Order and Princely Power*]

[17] Romaňák, Andrej. Stálá armáda a její vliv na sociální postavení poddaného lidu v Čechách. *Historie a vojenství* 32 [Standing Army and its Impact on the Social Status of Subjects in Bohemia. In: *History and Miltary*], 1983, vol. 2, p. 78. On the development of a standing army see Winkelbauer, Thomas: *Österreichische Geschichte 1522–1699. Teil 1: Ständefreiheit und Fürstenmacht*. Wien, 2003, pp. 416–420. [*Austrian History 1522-1699. Part 1: Free standing and Fürstenmach*]

[18] Saheb, Jan; Krůl, Martin. Nepravidelné ozbrojené útvary na Moravě a ve Slezsku v raném novověku. Valaši a jejich podíl na obraně zemských hranic. In: *Valašsko. Historie a kultura* [Irregular Armed Groups in Moravia and Silesia of the Early Modern Period. The Wallachians and their Role in Border Defence. In: *Wallachia. History and Culture*]. Ostrava, 2014, p. 156.

[19] Saheb, Jan. Zabezpečení moravských a slezských hranic v době Tökölyho povstání. In: *Kurucké vojny a ich odkaz v histórii, kultúre a umení/Kurucké války a jejich odkaz v historii, kultuře a umění* [Securing the Moravian and Silesian Borders at the time of the Thököly Uprising. In: *The Kuruc Wars and their Legacy in History, Culture, and Art*]. Dolný Kubín, 2011, pp. 67–78.

[20] Saheb, Jan. Protihabsburské stavovské povstání Imricha Tökölyho v Uhrách a obrana moravsko-slezsko-uherské hranice. *Slezský sborník* 2011, č. 3–4 [The Anti-Habsburg Uprising Led by Emeric Thököly in Hungary and the Defence of the Moravian-Silesian-Hungarian Border. In: *Acta Silesiaca*, 2011, vol. 3–4], p. 195.

[21] Zemský archiv v Opavě, pobočka Olomouc, *fond Arcibiskupství Olomouc*, inv. č., 182, sign. N 38 [Regional Archives in Opava, the

Olomouc branch, *The Olomouc Archbishopric Fund, inv.*, no. 182, file N 38].

[22] Saheb, Jan; Krůl, Martin. Nepravidelné ozbrojené útvary na Moravě a ve Slezsku v raném novověku. Valaši a jejich podíl na obraně zemských hranic. In: *Valašsko. Historie a kultura* [Irregular Armed Groups in Moravia and Silesia of the Early Modern Period. The Wallachians and their Role in Border Defence. In: *Wallachia. History and Culture*]. Ostrava, 2014, pp. 157–158.

[23] Saheb, Jan. Protihabsburské stavovské povstání Imricha Tökölyho v Uhrách a obrana moravsko-slezsko-uherské hranice. *Slezský sborník*, 2011, č. 3–4 [The Anti-Habsburg Uprising Led by Emeric Thököly in Hungary and the Defence of the Moravian-Silesian-Hungarian Border. In: *Acta Silesiaca*, 2011, vol. 3–4], p. 201.

[24] Drápala, Daniel. Portáši. Historie a tradice [The Portášes. History and Tradition]. *Brno*, 2017, pp. 11–21.

[25] *Moravský zemský archiv v Brně, fond A 8 – Zemská registratura, sign.*, p. 6, karton 814, 815 [*The Moravian Provincial Archive in Brno, fund A 8 – Provincial Filing*, sign., p. 6, coll. 814, 815].

[26] Drápala, Daniel. Portáši. Historie a tradice [The Portášes. History and Tradition]. *Brno*, 2017, pp. 57, 95–103, 111–112.

[27] Archiwum Państwowe w Katowicach oddział w Cieszynie, *fond Komora Cieszyńska, sign., 87*, pp. 52–63. [*State Archive in Katowice, Cieszyn branch, fond Cieszyńska Chamber, sign*]

[28] Saheb, Jan; Krůl, Martin. Nepravidelné ozbrojené útvary na Moravě a ve Slezsku v raném novověku. Valaši a jejich podíl na obraně zemských hranic. In: *Valašsko. Historie a kultura* [Irregular Armed Groups in Moravia and Silesia of the Early Modern Period. The Wallachians and their Role in Border Defence. In: *Wallachia. History and Culture*]. Ostrava, 2014, p. 159.

[29] Duncker, Carl von. *Oesterreichischer Erbfolge-Krieg 1740–1748*, II. Band. Wien 1896, pp. 116–118; Saheb, Jan: K průběhu 1. slezské války (1740−1742) na těšínsko-moravském pomezí. Těšínsko, 2006, č. 1 [The Course of the 1st Silesian War (1740-1742) on the Těšínsko-Moravian Border. In: *Těšínsko* 2006/1], p. 11−19.

[30] Drápala, Daniel. Portáši. Historie a tradice [The Portášes. History and Tradition]. *Brno*, 2017, pp. 95–103.
[31] Krůl, Martin; Saheb, Jan. Instrukce pro tzv. vybrance z roku 1715 (příspěvek k vojenským dějinám Těšínska). *Těšínsko*, 2015, č. 1 [Instructions for the so-called Vybranecs from 1715 (Contribution to the Military History of the Těšín Region). In: *Těšínsko*, 2015/1)], p. 75.
[32] *Národní archiv v Praze, fond Česká dvorská kancelář, sign. II A 3, karton*. 51 [*The National Archives in Prague, fund Cancellaria Aulica Bohemica, sign.* II A 3, f. 51].
[33] Krůl, Martin; Saheb, Jan. Instrukce pro tzv. vybrance z roku 1715 (příspěvek k vojenským dějinám Těšínska). *Těšínsko*, 2015, č. 1 [Instructions for the so-called Vybranecs from 1715 (Contribution to the Military History of the Těšín Region). In: Těšínsko 2015/1)], p. 83.
[34] Drápala, Daniel. Portáši. Historie a tradice [The Portášes. History and Tradition]. *Brno*, 2017, pp. 75–94.

BIOGRAPHICAL SKETCHES

Martin Krůl

Affiliation: Museum of the Těšín region

Education: Masaryk university of Brno

Research and Professional Experience: He is devoted to the history of Silesia in early modern times, focusing on the issues of military and fortifications. He regularly participate in international scientific conferences in the Czech Republic and abroad.

Professional Appointments: 2003–still: Museum of the Těšín region

Publications from the Last 3 Years:

Chapters in a collective monographs:

Krůl, Martin. Formy "kvartýrování" vojáků v raném novověku na příkladu Těšínska. In: R. Jež – D. Pindur et al. (eds.). Dům, palác a zámek vhmotné kultuře Slezska/Dom, pałac i zamek w kulturze materialnej Śląska, Cieszyńskie Studia Muzealne/*Těšínský muzejní sborník 6. Český Těšín 2018*, s. 197–218. [Forms of "quarrying" soldiers in early modern times on the example of Těšín. In: R. Jež - D. Pindur et al. (eds.). The House, Palace and Chateau of the Intangible Culture of Silesia / *House, the Palace and the Castle of the Cultural Material of Silesia*, Cieszynskie Studia Muzealne].

Krůl, Martin. Stavební vývoj kmenových táborů Teschen a počty jejich válečných zajatců. In: M. Krůl – J. Lusek et al. *ČAS – MÍSTA – LIDÉ. Systém nacistických táborů v letech druhé světové války*/CZAS – MIEJSCA – LUDZIE. Nazistowski systém obozowy w latach drugiej wojny światowej. Muzeum Górnośląskie w Bytomiu – Muzeum Těšínska: Bytom – Český Těšín 2017, s. 94–117. [Building development of the Teschen tribal camps and the numbers of their prisoners of war. In: M. Krul - J. Lusek et al. TIME - *PLACES - PEOPLE. The system of Nazi camps during the Second World War /* CZAS - MIEJSCA - LUDZIE. The Nazistowski system obozowy w latach drugiej wojny światowej. Museum of Górnośląskie w Bytomiu - Museum of Těšín: Bytom - Český Těšín 2017, pp. 94-117.].

Krůl, Martin. *Příklady využití historických pramenů a prospekčních metod k poznání minulosti jablunkovských šancí*. In: *Válečné události 17.–19. století z interdisciplinární perspektivy*. Praha 2018, just in print. [Examples of historical sources and prospective methods for understanding the past of Jablunkov chances. In: *War events 17-19. century from an interdisciplinary perspective*. Prague 2018,].

Krůl, Martin. *Skrze válku do evropského povědomí. Jablunkovské šance v korespondenci Dvorské válečné rady*. In: *Sborník k 70. narozeninám profesora Rudolfa Žáčka*. Opava 2018, just in print. [Through the War to European Conscience. Jablunkov chances in the correspondence of the War Council of the Dvor. In: *Proceedings for the 70th Birthday of Professor Rudolf Žáček*. Opava 2018].

Krůl, Martin. *Zásobování a stravování posádky na jablunkovských šancích v raném novověku. Příspěvek k problematice obživy v horských oblastech.* In: *Valašsko – historie a kultura II.*, Ostrava, 2018, just in print. [Supply and boarding crew on Jablunkov chances in early modern times. Contribution to Livelihoods in Mountain Areas. In: *Wallachia - History and Culture II.*, Ostrava, 2018].

Studies in professional journals:

Krůl, Martin; SAHEB, Jan. *Instrukce pro tzv. vybrance z roku 1715 (příspěvek k vojenským dějinám Těšínska)*. Těšínsko, 2015, č. 1, s. 73–88 [*Instructions for the so-called vybranci from 1715 (Contribution to the Military History of Těšín Region)*].

Krůl, Martin. *Vodovod na Velké šanci v Mostech u Jablunkova.* Těšínsko, 2015, roč. 58, č. 2, s. 1–14. [Wa*ter Duct to the Great Fort in Mosty u Jablunkova*].

Krůl, Martin. *Kníže Josef Václav Lichtenštejn "spiritus agens et movens" modernizace rakouského dělostřelectva.* Sborník prací Pedagogické fakulty Masarykovy univerzity, řada společenských věd. *Brno*, 2016, roč. 30, č. 1., s. 27–36. [*Prince Josef Václav Liechtenstein "spiritus agens et movens" modernization of Austrian artillery*. Proceedings of the Faculty of Education, Masaryk University, a number of social sciences. *Brno*, 2016, vol. 30, No. 1, pp. 27-36.].

Krůl, Martin. Obrana horských přechodů na Moravu a do Uher na příkladu hradeckých a jablunkovských šancí. *Archaeologia historica*, 2017, roč. 42, č. 2, s. 561–578. [Defense of mountain crossings in Moravia and Uher on the example of Hradec and Jablunkov chances. *Archaeologia historica*, 2017, roč. 42, No. 2, pp. 561-578.].

Jan Saheb

Affiliation: University of Ostrava

Education: PhD, Silesian university of Opava, doctoral degree program Czech and Czechoslovak history

Research and Professional Experience: He is devoted to the history of Moravia in early modern times, focusing on the issues of military, economic and social history. He is the author or co-author of a number of monographs (for example: the Hukvaldy estate in the period 1553–1619, in the context of the so called mensual estates of the Olomouc bishopric. Ostrava 2011; Career in the War of the Wars with the Ottoman Empire, Life of the Nobilized Knight Jan Němčický from Němčice 1555–1614. Ostrava 2017) and dozens of professional studies and popularizing articles. He also regularly participate in international scientific conferences in the Czech Republic and abroad.

Professional Appointments:

- 2008–2017 Museum of the Těšín region
- 2017–still Provincial Archives in Opava
- 2010–still University of Ostrava, Faculty of Arts, Department of History
- 2010–still University of Ostrava, Faculty of Arts, Centre for Economic and Social History

Web: https://ff.osu.eu/khi/jan-saheb/48179/#1-zakladni

Publications from the Last 3 Years:

Monographs:

Müller, Karel; Saheb, Jan. *Galerie erbů držitelů Paskova.* Paskov, 2018. [*Gallery of coats of arms of the owners of the Paskov Manor*].

Nováková, Lenka; Saheb, Jan. *Dějiny obce Trojanovice*. Ostrava, 2016. [*History of the village Trojanovice*].

Saheb, Jan, Müller, Karel. *Galerie držitelů Paskova.* Paskov, 2015. [*An overview of the owners of the Paskov estate*].

Saheb, Jan. *Dějiny Paskova.* Paskov, 2017. [*History of Paskov Manor*].

Saheb, Jan. *Kariéra ve víru válek s Osmanskou říší. Život nobilitovaného rytíře Jana Němčického z Němčic (1555–1614).* Ostrava, 2017. [*Career in the War of the Wars with the Ottoman Empire, Life of the Nobilized Knight Jan Němčický from Němčice 1555–1614*].

Chapters in a collective monographs:

Saheb, Jan. Církevní vrchnost a Židé na Moravě v raném novověku. In: *Šlechticův žid, žid šlechticem. Židovské elity a židovská šlechta v novověku a moderní době.* Ostrava – Częstochowa, 2015, s. 37–44. [Church Authority and Jews in Moravia in Early Modern Times. In: *Noble Jew, a Jew Jew. Jewish elites and Jewish nobility in modern times and modern times.* Ostrava - Częstochowa, 2015, pp. 37-44.].

Saheb, Jan. *Vzájemné styky českých zemí a Polska v raném novověku (1490–1740).* In: *Śladami Polaków na czeskim/austriackim Śląsku. Stopami Poláků v českém*/rakouském Slezsku. *Częstochowa* 2016, s. 33–37. [Intercourse between the Czech Lands and Poland in the Early Modern Age (1490-1740). In: *Śladami Polaków in czeskim / austriacim Śląsk. Traces of Poles in Czech* / Silesian Austria. *Częstochowa* 2016, p. 33-37.].

Saheb, Jan. *Hrabová součástí paskovského panství v letech 1538–1850.* In: *Historie obce Hrabová.* Dějiny, památky a osobnosti Hrabové od 13. století po současnost. *Ostrava*, 2017, s. 28–62. [Hrabová part of the Paskov manor house in the years 1538-1850. In: *History of Hrabová village.* History, monuments and personalities Hrabové from the 13th century to the present. *Ostrava*, 2017, p. 28-62.].

Saheb, Jan. *Strukturální proměny církevní správy Rakouského Slezska na prahu modernismu. K procesu transformace duchovní správy v 18. a první polovině 19. století*. In: *Modernizace církve od zrušení jezuitského řádu do II.* vatikánského koncilu. Ostrava, 2018, s. 54–66. [Structural transformations of the Church of Silesia on the threshold of modernism. The Process of Transformation of Spiritual Administration in the 18th and the First Half of the 19th Century. In: *Modernization of the Church from the abolition of the Jesuit Order to II.* Vatican Council. Ostrava, 2018, pp. 54-66.].

Saheb, Jan. Hrabě František Eusebius z Oppersdorfu ve sporu o moravsko-slezskou hranici v roce 1668. In: *Sborník k 70. narozeninám profesora Rudolfa Žáčka*. Opava, 2018, just in print. [Count Frantisek Eusebius of Oppersdorf in a dispute about the Moravian-Silesian border in 1668. In: Proceedings for the 70th birthday of Professor Rudolf Zacek. Opava, 2018, just in print].

Saheb, Jan. Polský původ moravské šlechty v díle genealoga Bartoloměje Paprockého z Hlohol. In: *Stopy polské šlechty v českých zemích v (raném) novověku*. Ostrava, 2018, just in print. [The Polish origin of the Moravian nobility in the work of the genealogist Bartholomew Paprocki of Hlohol. In: *Traces of Polish nobility in the Czech lands in (early) modern times*. Ostrava, 2018, just in print.].

Saheb, Jan; Solnický, Pavel. "Poslední století" Tvorkovských z Kravař. In: *Ad fontes. Sborník příspěvků věnovaných Ph Dr. Karlu Müllerovi k 60. narozeninám*. Opava, 2018, s. 85–109. [Solnický, Pavel. The Last Century of Tvorkov from Kravaře. In: *Ad fontes. Proceedings of papers dedicated to Ph. Karel Müller's 60th birthday*. Opava, 2018, pp. 85-109].

Studies in professional journals:

Krůl, Martin; Saheb, Jan. Instrukce pro tzv. vybrance z roku 1715 (příspěvek k vojenským dějinám Těšínska). *Těšínsko*, 2015, č. 1, s. 73–88 [Instructions for the so-called Vybranecs from 1715 (Contribution to the Military History of the Těšín Region)]

Saheb, Jan. *K procesu rekatolizace na Moravě v prvních desetiletích po tridentském koncilu (do roku 1619).* S přihlédnutím k poměrům na tzv.

mensálních statcích olomouckého biskupství. Sborník prací Pedagogické fakulty Masarykovy univerzity, řada společenských věd, *30*, 2016, č. 1, s. 14–26. [*The process of recatholization in Moravia in the first decades after the Council of Trident (until 1619).* Taking into account the relations on the so-called minor estates of the Olomouc bishopric. Proceedings of the Faculty of Education of the Masaryk University, series of social sciences, 30, 2016, No. 1, pp. 14-26.].

Saheb, Jan. Životní osudy "*soldáta*" Jana Němčického z Němčic. Ke klientelským vztahům a kariérním strategiím nižší šlechty v předbělohorském období, 1. část. *Těšínsko*, 2016, č. 1, s. 1–30. [The life of the soldier Jan Němčický from Němčice. On Clientele Relationships and Career Strategies of Lower Nobility, Part 1].

Saheb, Jan. Životní osudy "*soldáta*" Jana Němčického z Němčic. Ke klientelským vztahům a kariérním strategiím nižší šlechty v předbělohorském období, 2. *část. Těšínsko*, 2016, č. 2, s. 1–20. [The life of the soldier Jan Němčický from Němčice. On Clientele Relationships and Career Strategies of Lower Nobility, Part 2].

Saheb, Jan. Marginálie k dějinám západních Čech z let 1545–1568 v registrech korespondence olomouckých biskupů. *Bohemiae Occidentalis Historica*, *2*, 2016, č. 1, s. 77–84. [Marginals to the history of Western Bohemia from 1545-1568 in the correspondence registers of Olomouc bishops. Bohemiae *Occidentalis Historica*, 2, 2016, No. 1, pp. 77-84.Marginals to the History of Western Bohemia from the years 1545–1568 in the correspondence registers of Olomouc Bishops].

Saheb, Jan. *Normativní rámec temporální správy olomouckého biskupství v době sedisvakance v předbělohorském období.* Sborník prací Pedagogické fakulty Masarykovy univerzity, řada společenských věd, 30, 2016, č. 2, s. 34–42. [*Normative framework of the temporal administration of the Olomouc bishopric at the time of sedisvakance in the pre-Bleak period.* Proceedings of the Faculty of Education of Masaryk University, series of social sciences, 30, 2016, No. 2, pp. 34-42.].

Saheb, Jan. Působení rytíře Jana Němčického z Němčic na Vyškovsku. Skica ze života nižší šlechty před Bílou horou. *Vyškovský sborník*, 12,

2016, s. 51–90. [The influence of the knight Jan Němčický from Němčice in Vyškov. A sketch from the life of inferior nobility in front of the White Mountain. *Vyškovský sborník*, 12, 2016, s. 51-90].

Saheb, Jan. Kauza obležení paskovské tvrze v roce 1484. Beneš a Dobeš Černohorští z Boskovic v zápase o lenní statek Paskov. *Těšínsko*, 2017, č. 1, s. 1–14. [The cause of the siege of the Paskov fortress in 1484. Beneš and Dobeš Černohorští from Boskovice in the struggle for the Paskov farm. *Těšínsko*, 2017, No. 1, pp. 1-14.].

Saheb, Jan. Moravská epizoda v životě humanisty Ondřeje Dudiče z Hořehovice (1533–1589). Sborník prací Pedagogické fakulty Masarykovy univerzity, řada společenských věd, *31*, 2017, č. 2, s. 3–11. [The Moravian Episode in the Life of Humanist Ondřej Dudic of Hořehovice (1533–1589)].

Saheb, Jan. *Dopady třicetileté války na hmotné poměry šlechty v oblasti moravskoslezského pomezí (na příkladu Paskova).* In: Cieszyńskie studia muzealne/Těšínský muzejní sborník, *6*, 2018, s. 177–196. [*Impact of the Thirty Years' War on the Material Relations of the Nobility in the Moravian-Silesian Border Region*].

In: An In Depth Look at Hungary
Editor: Esperanta Rompa
ISBN: 978-1-53615-351-4

Chapter 4

NEW CRISIS – NEW ANSWERS

Attila Moizs, PhD
Faculty of Economic Science, Kaposvár University,
Kaposvár, Hungary

ABSTRACT

Since 2008 the Hungarian fiscal and monetary policy have been changed radically as a consequence of worldwide crisis. The new policy provided economic stability, but long-lasting cultural imbalance persisted. The renewed economic regulations managed several issues *pro futuro* but did not provide any solutions for the existing problem of debtors in Hungary. Although financial and economic reconstruction, the raising of the level of employment, the continuous cutdown of the prime interest rate, the lower interest of commercial banks and the higher GDP promoted the consolidation of the domestic loan market, they helped both individuals and enterprises, but the crash left behind a deep impact on Hungarian society. I guess neither the masses nor the State are getting ready for a new economic crisis, which is due to happen in the near future.

I strongly believe that a new economic crisis is going to result in sweeping changes in the Hungarian society. The study makes an attempt to prove that the financial knowledge of individuals, the level of the financial culture of a nation and mainly the convenient national/supranational financial regulation (including the state protection of consumers) determine fundamentally the situation of future generations. We have to see clearly that there is a close correlation between the financial (realized or failed) policy (legislation) and the structure of future society. The object of this study - focusing mainly on the monetary policy – is to demonstrate those instruments by which an excessively polarized society could be prevented in the near future.

INTRODUCTION

The Causes: Why Did the Last Worldwide Crisis Concern So Deeply the Hungarian Society in 2008 and Later?

There were a lot of causes which led to the disequilibrium of society and economy in the late of noughties, and some of them are worth identifying:

The explosion of crisis from 2008 found the Hungarian fiscal and monetary system in a grievously asymmetric, distorted position. The most emphatic features of its status were

- low the production capability of the national economy and high exposure to abroad,
- dependence of the public finance and national budget on creditors,
- the extremely liberal financial regulation of the banking system,
- the lack of early detection and warning systems,
- the unjustified optimism of the banking supervisory authorities,
- lower level of financial culture correlates with
- agents on the financial market who want to raise their consumption unwisely, also
- they had great confidence in the financial and monetary system
- and strong confidence in a neverending economic boom.

To prove the statements above – without detailed statistical figures – I try to expose the main characteristics of this issues with the help of some relevant facts and data. These numbers, values indicate well that the crisis found Hungary in a defenseless position at the end of 2008.

Low Production Capability of the National Economy and High Exposure to Abroad

The high external debt, the lost traditional and independent industry, the closing of mines, the unfinished reconstruction of the national agriculture, the remaining problems of privatization and reprivatization, the lack of exportable goods, products and services aggregately resulted in the weakness and dependency of Hungarian economy. Hungary had to import most of the products.

Hungary was ranked on the 51th place in the world rankings by GDP (nominal) per capita[1] in 2008, its performance was 15.569 USD. At the same time e.g., Romania had 10.160 USD, but the EU countries 39.038 USD, Germany 46.681 USD and USA 48.302 USD (1,49 EUR/USD currency).

Dependency of the Public Finance and National Budget on Creditors

The gross general government (Maastricht) debt[2] to GDP was one of the highest among the European countries (compared to the average of EU countries) in Hungary (71,6%), it was higher only in Belgium, Greece, Italy and Portugal. The gross external debt (loans from foreign bodies and sold funds abroad) was 6.994,73 billion HUF[3], it was 26% of GDP on 31st december 2008, almost all (6.774,83 billion HUF - 36.2 billion USD) in foreign currencies. In 2008 the deficit was 3,6 percentage of GDP, and some years later, in 2011 this ratio approximated the 5,5 percentage.

Thanks to the low level of economic performance, the financing of the budget was expensive and unpredictable, it depended on the expectation value of country risk, inflation and in a great part the high spreads were connected to the higher risk of clients and default risk charges. This time there was a critical period (2008-2011), when the risks increased exceptionally high, Hungary's credit rating fell and the investors escaped.

---

[1] Based on International Monetary Fund.

[2] This dataset presents statistics on government debt defined by the Maastricht Treaty, as the debt of the whole general government sector (gross, consolidated and nominal value).

[3] 37,4 billion USD - 187,19 HUF/USD exchange rate.

The exchange rates exploded, in the middle of July of 2008 1 USD was about 145 HUF, some months later (in March 2009) the rate was 249 HUF/USD. It meant that the nominal worth of external debt grew extraordinarily in the HUF-based budget.

The Extremely Liberal Financial Regulation of the Banking System

Without presentation of detailed regulation of Hungarian banking system, this paper focuses on some interesting facts to size up the Hungarian credit market and performance of commercial banks.

In 2008 the proportion of credits in foreign currencies (mainly in Swiss francs, euro) was 64,7% in Hungary opposite to other countries of this region (like Poland, Czech Republic and Slovakia), where the ratio stayed under forty percentage (9,1%-34,2%), but neither in Romania nor in Bulgaria was so high as the rate in Hungary. Both households and enterprises obtained loans in foreign currencies in spite of the fact that its earnings and incomes were available in Hungarian forints, therefore they tookon a huge bulge risk.

On the other hand, the then effective regulation did not prevent the banks from giving more loans than gathered client deposits. The credit/deposit rate was nearly 145 percentage (144,8% - the highest in the region), which meant that the banks hazarded much more than their owned capital and client liabilities. The awareness of the countries in the region, the acts and the practice resulted in significantly lower, moderate rates (Poland 114,8%, Czech Republic 82,8%, Slovakia 82,6%). The ratio of foreign liabilities was also the highest in Hungary (26,4%), contrasted to the countries mentioned above, these values balanced between 5,1%-10,5%.

The Lack of Early Detection and Warning Systems

The majority of specialists on the topic have the same opinion about this issue, namely before 2008, convenience and efficient warning system had not existed, which could have been able to recognize the problems of the banking system. But the immoderate expansion of banking credit stocks and the spread of the less stable derivate reliabilities (instead of safer and durable traditional client deposits) did warn the supervisory authorities. There was not an organization (including the government and the entire state which could have warned the customers and debtors to avoid the excessive indebtedness, mainly in foreign currencies.

Table 1. Loans for Households (Billion HUF and %)

Year	2000	2001	2002	2003	2004	2005	2006	2007	2008
Billion HUF	768	1.163	1.933	3.116	4.053	5.089	6.111	7.447	9.621
Growth %		51,4	66,2	61,2	30,7	25,6	20,1	21,9	29,2

Some datas of the International Monetary Fund help to prove the above mentioned statement about the changes of loans given to households in this period.

These values present an obviously riskful progress, but there was not an accomplished model or point of reference, which could show the critical value, the sector was out of recommendations and adequate rules.

The Unjustified Optimism of the Banking Supervisory Authorities

The supervisory authorities, the *Hungarian Financial Supervisory Authority* and the *Hungarian National Bank* could not detect disequilibrium which appeared at that time (particularly from 2005 to 2008) in the Hungarian banking sector (and worldwide), and as they could not understand the causes of the loss of equilibrium, they stayed inactive.

Although the Hungarian Financial Supervisory Authority gave a summary about the worldwide financial situation in its annual report in 2006 [1] but it was not deliberate enough:

> "While the vulnerability of the global macroeconomic boom apparently remains at medium level, it is slightly decreasing due to the strict monetary actions taken. With a view to the interest cycle, the expectations for the global bond market have improved significantly.
>
> In 2007, the EUR/USD exchange rate, which can be considered the most important product of foreign currency markets, may change

depending on minor asymmetries in the expected slowdown of European and North American economies. From this respect, no major correction seems necessary. The currencies of developing economies are efficiently strengthened by the high volume of direct capital influx. Their volatility, however, will remain significant due to the fluctuating nature of portfolio investments. One serious risk in the coming period may be the extensive accumulation of global carrytrade funds. The low-interest-rate source currency in these funds is mainly the Japanese yen or the Swiss franc. Any revaluations of these currencies may cause significant losses. In the case of the Swiss franc, the debtors of foreign currency loans taken out in Hungary would also be impacted significantly."

The supervisors thought that the market processes, the rule of demand and supply would resolve the balance problems, and prevailed the "laisser fair, laisser passer" principle, but they did not take any of these factors into account:

- the competition between commercial banks and cooperative banks did not bear a relation to interest rates, it was a risk competition, where the winner was the one who took a higher jeopardy,
- contracts among a bank and its customer were rather asymmetric, unilateral rights for banks were secured in substantial points of agreement (e.g., raise interest), foreign exchange risk and costs were devolved to clients,
- the rising prices of estates was not based on real market rates, they were determined by the expectations,
- the labor market was insecure, a lot of workplaces ceased to exist, the new employers were sometimes short-lived, hence the incomes of households could not be calculated.

Lower Level of Financial Culture

The Hungarian educational system did not emphasise the importance of financial knowledge and the educational institutions did not teach the basics of economics. People, especially the most of rural individuals did not posess the basic knowledge indispensable for participating in economic life, enforcing their rights, understanding the consequences of their decisions to calculate the future results of their action. It was quite an unequal combat between uninformed customers and professional banks. Most of the people and the managers of small businesses were incapable of calculating interestes, comprehending the risk of foreign currencies in a loan contract, or detecting the assymetric conditions of the change of interest, exchange rates and covers given.

A Hungarian foundation entrusted GFK Hungary with sizingup the financial knowledge and culture of the adult population in the country based on OECD methodology [2]. The period monitored began in 2010, and the main results of the survey were summarized by the following statements:

- The ratio of households making any budget about their costs and incomes was 32 percentage,
- Approx. 60 percentage of the inhabitants said that three months was the longest period till they could maintain their household without their salaries,
- 33 percentage of them declared to choose financial services, that they did not consider any other offers or options during their decision.

Agents on the Financial Markets Who Want to Raise Their Consumption Unwisely

Having loans does not mean a problem in a healthy and balanced economy, the conscious customer is able to determine the convenience degree of credits and responsibilities but on the low level of financial culture, like in Hungary at that time, increasing indebtedness could be dangerous.

The loss or decrease of salaries and other incomes requires its supplements, and the simpliest way seemed to get a new or bigger loan, in spite of the fact that due to the growing client risk, the banks gave their money more expensively than earlier. As the exchange rates were allowed to change and taking into consideration that not only spreads but also the prime rates (interest) became higher, a large-scale of customers and small or medium-sized enterprises got into a debttrap.

Great Confidence in the Financial and Monetary System

Traditions of the previous political system, the dictatorial state did not let the self-determination and self-reliance of its citizens, therefore the individuals got into the habit of preordinated ways. In fact, it was a coercion, but on the other hand it was a smooth manner to attain personal (or economic) goals. The undue strictness was replaced by economic and political liberalism, which abolished the barriers and both the people and the state just began to learn the new era. The indivuals tried to find the borderlines of freedom and the state tried to create the frame of its own comptency and limits of duties. In spite of proper intentions the state was notable to turn into a "provident and helping state" and the people who believed in itbecame soon disappointed.

> The Hungarian National Bank published a Report on financial stability in October 2008 [3] that "the Hungarian financial system is stable and has a substantial capital buffer in international comparison, which increases its resilience to risks." And "The interbank market is functioning smoothly, and there is adequate forint liquidity in the financial system. There has been no sign of deterioration in foreign currency liquidity, neither in the form of a freezing of markets nor due to withdrawals of funds provided by parent banks." This month the official 3-months BUBOR rates jumped from 8,73% to 11,87%.

The national Treasury Department and banking supervisory authorities played the lead in this issue, who had the knowledge, opportunity, possibility and instruments to check, prevent and arrest the unfavorable running.

Strong Confidence in a Neverending Economic Boom

At the turn of the centuries people experienced that they could easily obtain real estate loans and the banks gave them apparently relatively cheap credits in foreign currencies. The interests offered were smaller on the domestic financial market than ever before thanks to the loans which were available in major foreign currecies (USD, Euro, CHF, JPY). Since the prices on the housing market were growing permanently, they hoped the prices would hit the level of Western Europe. Nevertheless, the Hungarian forint interests resulted in higher yields for investors, therefore they did not seek alternative possibilities to place their money, like forint-based traditional deposits, growingly combined funds and forint-based stocks. But a considerable part of debtors and investors didnot take into account the changes of the financial, housing and manpower markets, took no notice of currency volatility. People took up a comfortable position and did not want to think over their investment strategy and there was not any prediction which would have urged them to do it. In 2007 the Authorithy surveyed the overall risk environment in Hungary in its annual report [4] referring to 2006, but it was not a real and sufficient warning either:

> "Besides the expectedly favorable long-term effects, the correction to the state budget that was started in 2006 will also make a negative impact on financial mediation on the short run which must be taken into consideration as well. The growth opportunities of financial institutions will diminish which may lead to a higher ratio of risky lending deals. It may cause difficulties to institutions, mainly to small ones that are less proficient in risk management. What it means is that the macroeconomic environment in 2007 is also burdened by significant risks for financial mediation which calls for special diligence and care on the part of financial market players.
>
> The significant improvement of the economic equilibrium brought about by fiscal corrections also has a favorable effect on short-term trends. It may principally show in the stabilisation of sovereign loan rating, improved conditions for external financing, reduced yield expectation for government bonds and the reduced vulnerability of the Hungarian currency. This process has already begun in the second part of 2006 and is expected to continue in 2007, provided corrective measures are sustained. As a result of falling domestic demand, the inflationary pressure may decrease during the rest of the year, which renders a positive outlook for the forint bond market."

One year later the Hungarian Financial Supervisory Authority highlighted [5] the following indication about the risk impact on the financial sector:

> "Further significant losses should be expected within and beyond the financial sector and the crisis is quite likely to linger on for an uncertain period of time. What it also means is that we should continue to expect symptoms like high risk premiums on money and corporate bond markets, a high degree of volatility onfinancial markets, especially on stock and foreign currency markets and a lower global risk appetite that strikes developing markets more than other markets. All this means that liquidity will remain expensive and market risks will stay high in the long run."

The state did not take these reports seriously, and the prognosis was not followed by a legislative act. Neither the state nor banks thought about to reserve enough money to tide over hard times.

The Hungarian National Bank recognized the problems [6], but at the end of 2008 it was too late for the actors of the domestic financial system:

> "Until now domestic banks have tried to maintain profitability by boosting their lending portfolios, and this is associated with increased risk-taking. The fact that credit standards are now no longer being eased and the rise in lending interest rates indicates that the intensity of risk-based competition is no longer increasing. On the other hand, the availability of loans with high LTV ratios, the emergence of increasingly risky products (e.g., unit-linked insurance combined with a foreign currency loan) and the growth in sales via brokers suggest that intense risk-based competition continues. Inadequately trained brokers with improper incentives may contribute to over-indebtedness and, through sales to less creditworthy customers, to increasing credit risk."

It summarized that the state, its bodies, the customers and mainly the entire monetary system were not ready for the challenges of the changing macroeconomic environment. There were a lot of phenomena in Hungary which forecast the expected effects of the crisis in 2008, and it seems that they have appeared before as well, therefore it is our responsibility to show them.

The Present: How Did the Changes Transform the Hungarian Economy and Society as a Result of the Reformed Fiscal and Monetary Policy of the State?

Production Capability of the National Economy and Exposure to Abroad

The new government recognized that high external debt caused huge enonomic and political dependency on other countries, mostly the European Union countries, therefore it started to search for new possibilities to grow the national export and decrease the ratio of external financing in budget estimates.

During the 2014-2020 budgetary period the European Union granted 34 billion EUR (about 9.000 billion HUF) as a development fund to Hungary. Hungary spent up to the end of 2018 about 31% of it, being the leader in its region in this respect, where the average ratio was 27%. It means that Hungary spent 2.000 – 2.500 billion HUF during these years, and in 2009 budgetary year the payment planned for domestic actors was 1.996 billion HUF, while the demand was 1.359 billion HUF from the EU, therefore the balance payments. Resulted in a debit of 596 billion HUF.

Although the BMW Group announced that following the Audi and Mercedes-Benz they would establish a new car factory in Hungary in 2019[4]. At the end of 2017 the automotive industry provided about 5 percentage of GDP and 34 percentage of the total export of the country and the latter one may reach 40% within reasonable time. The number of employees in the car industry converged to 180.000 capita. But during the last years the growth of Hungarian motor industry slowed down and the results of the sector were worse than EU averages.

The growth of service industries played a crucial role in progression of GDP, thanks mostly to the extremely high level of employment[5], which contributed to the rise of domestic conpsumption.

---

[4] The car making will begin probably in 2023.

[5] 69,5% on 30th September 2018.

By the end of 2017 Hungary was on the 58th place in the world rankings by GDP (nominal) per capita (earlier 51th) despite the fact that its GDP grew from 27.186,6 to over 38.355,1 billion forints in this interval.

Although these datas are promising in fact, and a lot of the growth rates are better than in most European countries, we have to consider the convenient basis. What the point of reference is truly convenient like? Although the averages of EU obviously provide a good point of reference, but the best templates are the countries of the closest region, the states (e.g., Poland, Slovakia, Czech Republic, Romania) which possess similar qualities.

The main issues and challenges of the present are the decrease of the rural population, which is in close relation with the unresolved problems of the structure of agriculture, furthermore with the situation of the operation of the labour market. The population of the countryside impoverishes and aims at moving to closer cities. But the migration does not stop at national frontiers. The European Economic and Monetary Union (EMU) secures the citizens of the EU to undertake work in any of its countries, which means that the salaries and benefits in other European countries determine or influence the Hungarian employment market to a great extent at least from two respects. On one hand, the migration of qualified workers causes shortage of labor in Hungary and on the other hand, the employers have to pay more and more to theirs workers.

Another significant issue is that taxes and dues still amount to more than 40 percentage of the estimates of total incomes (19 580 billion HUF) in the 2019 budgetary year.

Dependence of the Public Finance and National Budget (Public Finance) on Creditors

Altough the GDP increased about 41 percentage, the Maastricht debt rose to 52 percentage in this period (from 19.465,6 billion HUF to 29.535,4 billion HUF) therefore the gross government debt to GDP was 73,3% at Q2 in 2018, compared to 71,6% in 2008.

The gross external debt was 6.165 billion HUF on 31st October 2018 (it was about 12% lower than in 2008), 5.765 billion HUF in foreign currencies[6] (it was about 15% lower than in 2008). However, the ratio of external debt/Maastricht debt improved in fact from 2008 to 2018, but the result was really thanks to the faster growth of internal debt.

The deficit to GDP might have been about 2,4% in 2018 without an ongoing account with the EU (it was about 23% lower than in 2008).

The exchange rate was 280,94 HUF/USD at the end of 2018, which was nearly doubled compared to ealier (in the middle of July of 2008) rates.

The undermentioned publication of Reuters [7] illustrated well the dependency of Hungary on the EU:

> "A delay in reimbursements of billions of euros has already increased Hungary's cash-flow budget deficit and a row over payments could worsen relations with the EU that has threatened to impose sanctions on a country it accuses of flouting EU rules on democracy, civil rights and corruption."

Changes of the Financial Regulation

The regulation of credit-, insurance- and investment markets altered radically after 2008 in Hungary. The changes focused on two main objects: firstly, they tried to arrange the unsustainable situation of debtors, who were suffering from the previous regulation, secondly, they created convenient rules for example in the relationships of banks and theirs clients. A part of them were retroactive (e.g., the *Act XXXVIII of 2014 on the Resolution of Questions Relating to the Uniformity Decision of the Curia Regarding Consumer Loan Agreements of Financial Institutions*, or the Act XL of 2014 on the rules of account connected to the the Act XXXVIII of 2014), which changed the legal positions of the debtors and creditors *ex tunc*. They inhibited the banks from applying exchange margins, raising the interest rates unilaterally, and obliged them to charge back amounts that debtors had paid earlier upon these titles.

---

[6] These are only 21,5 billion USD and 20,1 billion USD because the current exchange rate was 286,4 HUF/USD in October 2018 compared to 187,19 HUF/USD in 2008.

Another part of laws established strict rules *pro futuro* for demanding and giving credits mostly in case of individuals and households, for instance they determined the minimal ratio of incomes/monthly installments and determined the maximum of applicable interest rates additionally to abolish the possibility of unilateral interest growing (Act CLXII of 2009 on the lent credits for customers, 32/2014. (IX. 10.) HNB decree on the regulation of income-rated installment).

This change of regulation coincided with other fundamental legislative acts, like the creation of the new Constitution (Fundamental Law of Hungary, 2011), Civil Code (The Act V/2013), and a new Act on Credit Institutions and Financial Enterprises (CCXXXVII/2013, hereafter Credit Institution Law), new Act LXXXVIII of 2014 on the Business of Insurance and new Act CXXXIX of 2013 on the Hungarian National Bank.

Besides the national level of legislation, the Hungarian fiscal and monetary policy have to consider the level of supranational laws, the acts and regulations which origin from international law or are based on the legal basis of the EU:

- Decisions of the European Summits of The Hague (1969), Paris (1972), Brussels (1978), Hanover (1988), Madrid and Strasbourg (both 1989), and Maastricht (1991-1992),
- Articles 119-144, 219 and 282-284 of the Treaty on the Functioning of the European Union (TFEU),
- Protocols annexed to the TFEU on the transition to the third stage of economic and monetary union, the excessive deficit and macroeconomic imbalances procedures, the convergence criteria, and the European System of Central Banks and the European Central Bank.

The obligations determine the framework of Hungarian fiscal and monetary policy, they were ratified on the national level. For example, some of the Stability and Growth Pact's rules aim to prevent fiscal policies from heading in potentially problematic directions, while others are there to correct excessive budget deficits or excessive public debt burdens.

Although Hungary is not a member of the Banking Union[7] there are rules which directly form part of Hungarian laws - like Directive 2013/36/EU of the European Parliament and of the Council of 26 June 2013 on access to the activity of credit institutions and the prudential supervision of credit institutions and investment firms, and Regulation (EU) No 575/2013 of the European Parliament and of the Council of 26 June 2013 on prudential requirements for credit institutions and investment firms – and the State is responsible for observancy.

The Lack of Early Detection and Warning Systems

The crisis proved that the monetary, fiscal and macroecomomic imbalances correlated strongly with the national economies of EU's Member States, therefore the European Union intended to ensure the EU countries to withstand future crises through economic and social reforms and responsible fiscal and monetary policies. For this purpose a new economic EU governance based on monitoring, prevention and correction was established and strenghtened. .

In addition, the European Commission produces the Alert Mechanism Report (AMR) that help to identify potential economic imbalances and other economic problems using a scoreboard of selected indicators and determine the necessary policy action. Depending on its conclusions the macroeconomic imbalance procedure (MIP) [8] may be ordered.

The AMR 2018 of Comission [9] contains country-specific commentaries about imbalances, risks and adjustment. It states:

> "the previous round of the MIP, no macroeconomic imbalances were identified for Hungary" and "the economic reading highlights issues relating to the housing market and labor market, although risks appear contained. The Commission will at this stage not carry out further in-depth analysis in the context of the MIP."

---

[7] The banking union is an EU-level banking supervision and resolution system which operates on the basis of EU-wide rules. It aims to ensure that the banking sector in the euro area and the wider EU is safe and reliable and that non-viable banks are resolved without recourse to taxpayers' oney and with minimal impact on the real economy.

Concerning the Hungarian banking system it must be mentioned that it basically depends on the EU regulations, and mostly the European Central Bank, which sets and governs the monetary policy and oversees its execution Europe-wide.

However, the banking system of the EU has not got over its losses yet, as Josef Ackermann mentioned in an interview [10] published by the Financial Times (on 3rd January 2019) *"Europe suffers from the sorry state of its banks."* He warns that 10 years after the financial crisis in the USA, the United States's dominance prevails on the global capital markets, its banks are more profitable and healthier, whilst the banks of the Eurozone (and obviously other European banks), mainly the investment bank, are in a regretful position.

The Country Report of Hungary 2018 [11], which was created within the framework of European Semester and based on the estimates of facts and datas, can be comprehended as a kind of detection and warning system. Regarding the Hungarian banking system the Report contains some important conclusions:

- The state remains an active player in the financial sector. It maintains a high presence across the sector and is proceeding slowly with privatisation. The state continues to be a majority shareholder in a few local commercial banks. It also owns the fast-growing Eximbank whose lending business goes beyond its traditionally supported export activity of corporates. At the same time, the Hungarian Development Bank and the financial arm of the state-owned Hungarian Post are expanding their lending activities by targeting SMEs and retail clients. The state remains the main shareholder of the Budapest Stock Exchange (BSE) through the central bank. Given that the BSE is also supervised by the central bank, the current ownership setup raises governance issues.
- The government also promotes the domestic ownership of banks. This process and high government involvement in the banking sector create new challenges for the banking supervision. As the experiences of other countries in the region also show, these types

of banks are more vulnerable to corporate governance problems, which in turn can lead to problems with credit allocation, credit risk control and asset quality.

- The efficiency of the Hungarian banking sector remains an issue. The banking sector has shed a fourth of its branches since 2008 and operates with 11% less staff. However, the economy remains overbanked in EU comparison. The uptake of digital banking services is one of the lowest in the EU. The banking sector struggles to hire experts to bolster their digital arms. The operating expenses of Hungarian banks amounted to over 3% of total assets on average at the end of 2016, unchanged since 2015. The cost-to-income ratio is close to 74%, over 10 pps. Higher than the already high average of euro area banks and 20 pps. Higher than some of the regional peers. Low efficiency of the sector may give rise further consolidation.

Besides these factors other significant issues exist concerning the Hungarian banking system, which are not mentioned above:

- It seems that within a few years the sector will lose traditional branches, which actually give most of their income. The deposit accounts and other forms of savings in fact did not carry real interests thanks to financial environment, fees, taxes and inflation. Depositors turn to alternative forms of reserves, like real estates and combined funds. The fees of current accounts, like bank transfers and charges of transfers are costlier than the costs of new transfer payment systems and startups. The state maintains the transactional fees, which were introduced to supplement the budget, but it causes extra fees for banks. Since the banks devolved these costs to clients, theirs services came uncompetitive compared to banks in surrounding countries.
- According to the Report, the government has the intention to hold the bigger part of banking sector in domestic hands. Thanks to the reallocation, the shares of properties came to be concentrated,

therefore the capability of capital accumulation and supplement decreased undoubtedly. In addition, the state created the *Act on the integration of cooperative credit institutions and the modification of certain legal regulations* (Act CCXXXVII/2013) and practically eliminated the Hungarian cooperative banking sector. It means a great problem because, thanks to its conservative business policies, the savings cooperative sector remained stable and liquid, even during the time of crisis, hence cooperatives could be main actors in the process of the abolishment of social and economical differences. Consequently, it is very important that the legislative system does not consider savings cooperatives to be economic organizations, but rather *countervailing power* [12], which are able to merge the economical functions with cultural, social and community building functions.

Changes of the Banking Supervisory Authorities

Bankruptcies and the position of the whole banking sector of Hungary pointed out at the turn of the centuries that the quality and coverage of supervision over financial institutions were insufficient. The optimism was replaced by the concern for collapse. Initially the supervisory authorities were busy with the assesment and arrangement of damages, afterwards they tried to create a new approach and treatment of the financial sector.

Since it was typical of almost the entire European banking sector (and worldwide as well), the Hungarian legislation ratified the supranational regulation in its national law, the adaptation of directives and regulations called for a new structure of supervision. Therefore, the Act CXXXIX of 2013 on the Hungarian National Bank terminated the double check of the sector, the Hungarian Financial Supervisory Authority was merged into the Hungarian National Bank, and became a "super authority," with functions of a central bank, which leads and executes the monetary policy, a licencer, supervisory and resolution authority and it had also a legislative function to create regulations on the supervised sector. It is a consumer protection organization, and by means of "unorthodox" tools supports the fiscal policy of the government actively, including the acceleration of the economy, besides being a member of the *Financial Stability Council*.

> "According to the Central Bank Act, the basic tasks of the Magyar Nemzeti Bank (hereinafter referred to as 'MNB') has expanded in point of maintaining and strengthening financial stability, on the other hand new instruments are available for these new tasks. Within this framework the Financial Stability Council of MNB has been established on 1st October, 2013. The Financial Stability Council is a decision-making body of the MNB established by the new Central Bank Act (Act CXXXIX of 2013 on Magyar Nemzeti Bank), and its scope of competence includes, within the strategic framework defined by the Monetary Council, the decision-making concerning the tasks specified..." [13]

The Financial Stability Council *inter alia*

- continuously monitor the stability of the system of financial intermediation as a whole and of the financial markets including international markets,
- analyse and take account of risk factors threatening the system of financial intermediation as a whole,
- discuss strategic, regulatory and risk-related issues affecting the system of financial intermediation as a whole and issues opinions if necessary,
- in situations threatening the stability of the system of financial intermediation as a whole, assess systemic risks and decide on the required tools,
- discuss the recommendations and decisions issued by the European Supervisory Authorities and the European Systemic Risk Board as needed,
- annually define the priority target areas of the MNB's control activities,
- make decisions in administrative proceedings relating to the exercise of supervision over persons, bodies and activities and its resolution function.

Lower Level of Financial Culture

The first part of the chapter demonstrated the main results of an OECD-based survey referring to the year 2010, the following statements below refer to 2015[8]:

- The ratio of households who made any budget about their costs and incomes fell from 32 to 25 percentage,
- Furthermore 60 percentage of the population said that three months was the longest period till they could maintain their household without their salary,
- In 2015 22 percentage of them declared to choose financial services and they did not consider other offers and potentials during decision compared to 33 percentage in 2010.
- Certain products examined – namely insurance, current accounts and credit cards were not better known (or in a slight measure) than earlier. Only in the case of stocks a higher ratio was noticed, in 2015 the 79% of pollees knew the meaning of stock opposite to 65%, which was measured five years before.
- The proportion of people who gave correct answers to the test questions orally on financial elements indicated a decreasing tendency in this cycle based on the survey. At more difficult tasks, like interest and yield calculation of funds or investments the number of proper answers was lower.

The survey concluded that the scrutinies revealed the long-term approach of the population to spend and invest money, and the clear tendency was that people came less conscious, careful and previsional.

The Money Compass Fund which comissioned the GFK with the survey mentioned above founded by the Hungarian National Bank, the Hungarian Banking Association and the Student Loan Centre Ltd. It indicated that both the state and the banking sector put emphasis on the education of the present and mostly the next generations, but irrespectively of their intention, the low

[8] They are the latest datas available.

level of financial culture will cause issues in the immediate future of Hungary.

Existence of Masses on the Financial Markets Who Want to Raise Their Consumption Unwisely

In November of 2018 the KSH [14] published suprising data about the growth of economy in Hungary, GDP in the last (third) quarter rose unexpectedly by about 5%. The power of enlargement was the consumption of households thanks to the high level of employment and the higher salaries (which was on average one thousand EUR, about 1.140 USD). In addition, the ratio of loans was 13,9% regarding enterprises and 5,21% concerning households in the year before 30th September 2018. In this period the growth of consumption regarding households was 4,7%, the average consumer price index was 2,8% in 2018.

In view of these facts it seems that the rise of consumption does not only have a basis, but it is prosperous and even sustainable development is needed.

Great Confidence in the Financial and Monetary System

Undoubtedly, the government and the Hungarian National Bank made a lot of decisions and created several Acts and Decrees which helped to stabilize the economy beyond 2008, moreover they have managed to set the economy on a growing line by now. Some of these decisions and laws left neither the banking system nor the legal system untouched, as a consequence, they definitely concerned the position of households and SME's. The everyday life of debtors – especially who had loans in foreign currencies – radically changed, a lot of people lost their properties and along with it the reliance on the state for a long time to come.

The conjuncture index usually gives a good approach to confidence and shows the proper measure of satisfaction and exceptations of a society. In Hungary the change was radical: the business confidence index developed substantively from -16,3 to + 15,4 during the period between 2012 and 2018, the consumer confidence index grew from -56,6 to -10,6 in the same time, and the conjuncture index increased from -26,8 to +8,6 by GKI[9] [15]. The results of the survey reflects strong optimism.

In favor of clairvoyance – in this case – any poilitical issues cannot be avoided, seeing that people frequently blame the current Government of thestate. The governing parties are supported actually by 35% of the constituents[10] and this ratio has been exceptionally high for a long time as a result for example the measures taken for debtors or the friendly degree of interest and the guaranteeing increasing minimum wage. The good data of budget and the improving national economic performance in effect allow us to have confidence in the future.

Although the convenience and effective monetary measures and the "strong arm" of the Hungarian National Bank mended the reputation of the sector, but based on a survey, only one among 4 person trusts the Hungarian banking system nowadays. Incidentally, the subsequent on-going decrease of bank branches – particularly with regard to saving cooperatives – abolishes those traditional connections that helped to support the trust between the bank and the customer.

Strong Conviction in a Neverending Economic Boom

The Parliament and Government created several preventive rules to keep debtors in bounds. The low level of interests worldwide are beneficial only for a while, later it blocks the accumulation of capital and eventuates extreme and unequal consumption. Thanks to the national and supranational legislation and the close unpleasant experiences the Hungarian National Bank prepared hard for new challenges, and also the reserves are higher than before.

There are some signs and trends which forecast the eventuality bust, but the actors of financial market didnot indicate their comprehension. The press plays an important role in incomprehension because it gives assymetryc

---

[9] The business confidence index is calculated based on answers and expectations about volumen of outputs, turnovers and employment in branches of industry (included buliding and service industries) and trade. The consumer confidence index is calculated based on answers and expectations about financial situation of households, the economic situation of the country and outlooks of saving markets.

[10] Based on *Századvég Alapítvány*.

information about the position of the national economy with the help of public channels and other close organs. On one hand they emphasize the truly great results of fiscal and monetary policy, on the other hand they do not pay enough attention to present the structural problems of the economy and the sensible marks of imbalances. For this reason a significant part of people may think that the national economy is strong enough to struggle with the troubles itself. The most of the people didnot read the reports of the Hungarian National Bank unfortunately, although the consistently published e.g., Macroprudential reports, Public Finance reports, Financial Stability reports, Growht reports, and Financial Consumer Protection reports give sufficient and reliable evaluation about the domestic economic position and outlooks.

The current data of consumption and the improving conjuncture index confirm that the society has not been ready yet for tiding over a new economic crisis.

Another warning signal came from the EU. The European Commision published [16] a full set of macroeconomic forecasts for the EU and its Member States in autumn (November) 2018. Referring to Hungary the paper estimated the next values.

Table 2. Indicators and values (%)

Indicators	2017	2018	2019	2020
GDP growth (%, yoy)	4,1	4,3	3,4	2,6
Inflation (%, yoy)	2,4	3,0	3,3	3,0
Unemployment (%)	4,2	3,6	3,3	3,2
Public budget balance (% of GDP)	-2,2	-2,4	-1,9	-1,8
Gross public debt (% of GDP)	73,3	72,9	70,3	68,6
Current account balance (% of GDP)	3,0	1,2	-0,0	0,3

Based on the forecast the Commission expects:

> “Economic growth is set to slow down after a strong 2018 as the domestic business cycle matures, fiscal stimulus gradually moderates, and headwinds from the global economy strengthen.”

In spite of the fact that the data in general show signs of improvement, the fall of GDP growth and the unaltered high level of public debt predict an uncertain future.

THE FINDINGS AND PROPOSALS

The significant findings of this chapter and the proposals which may assist to solve these issues can be summarized as follows:

- *Issue 1:* The participants of the Hungarian economic life are under-informed concerning the changes and dangers of national and worldwide economy.
- *Issue 2:* The actors cannot experience the real performance of the economy, the reference points do not fit in all cases.
- *Issue 3:* It is difficult to judge if the granted opportunities and possibilities by the EU and the boom are exploited sufficiently. There are a lot of distorting effects, like the allocation of subventions of the EU, or the persistent winners of statal open biddings, which are the obstructions of the conformation to an efficient and competitive sector. A determining part of the economic elite is specialized for statal orders and if the accomplished investments are as efficient as required.
- *Issue 4:* However, the government emphasised the importance of economic independence and evidently improved the construction and amount of external debt but Hungary's position essentially did not change only transformed: furthermore it depends on the EU's subventions and rules, also the performance and outputs of automotive industries worldwide. The trade war between the USA and China may carry new hazards for the Hungarian economy because of export dependence.
- *Issue 5:* The restructuring of the economy still has to be waited for: the high ratio of taxes in estimate of budgetary incomes causes the exceptionally vulnerability of public finance, hence of the economy.

Regarding the appropriation of expenditure, the main problems are unaltered: the huge suppliers (pension fund and social insurance) are underfunded and their services are insufficient.

- *Issue 6: "Economic growth is set to slow down after a strong 2018,"* but the government and the Hungarian National Bank applied all substantial fiscal and monetary leverage for economic development.
- *Issue 7:* The determination of the ratio among public functions and designation of the public purposes: for example in accordance with the spirit of the Constitution, we have to take care of the health of the present and the next generations alike. The current problems of the social and the healthcare systems will visibly cause a lot of trouble already in the near future.
- *Issue 8:* The social gaps are growing larger. In spite of higher wages, the difference among social strata is on the rise, instead of the widening of the middle-class, new fault-lines appeared in Hungarian society, the different stratification of the population according to more critera can be observed. Incomes and so thus the standards of living are changing diversely depending on sources of incomes (public servants, pensioners, employees of the competitive sector, foreign country, subsidies) or locations (capital, other cities, countryside, west or east part of the Country, foreign country, etc.) The impoverishment menace is more than 25% of the citizens (about 2,5 million people) meanwihle the wealth of a small group is increasing to an unimaginable extent. It seems that the historical chance to realize the idea of an expanded and affluent middle class has temporarily failed.
- *Issue 9:* The symptoms and distortions which characterize the economy and society nowadays will determine the habits and character of the next generations, therefore the present values and faults of society bears upon the economic progression in the following decades. Only a performance-orinted society is capale of training up those young people with whom the effective economy is sustainable.
- *Issue 10:* Although there is not a correct register, different sources estimate about 600.000 citizens who are working at present in other EU countries for a shorter or longer period of time. This kind of migration

causes serious problems already at the current 3,6% level of unemployment rate, it will come to critical at the estimated levels.

Furthermore:

- *Proposal 1:* Economic information has to be broadened and updated. All instruments, the media, liquid assets are available for the state to give preventive and adequate information about the current and potential dangers of the economy, but the degree of capacity utilization is relatively exiguous. At every level of education it is needed to teach financial knowledge, which may help to impove the financial culture of the people.
- *Proposal 2*: The avoidance of the sweeping reform of the social insurance system will cause inestimable injury and today it is a convenient matter. The realisation the support of mass sport are indispensable for the lifelong physical and mental balance of people who are (or will be) the supreme part of the manpower market.
- *Proposal 3:* We have to explore the causes which motivate people to leave the counrty and think over how the state can help them to be succesful in Hungary.
- *Proposal 4:* If Hungary takes the closing up to Western Europe seriously, it has to be started in the restructuring of the economy immediately. The differences are growing continuously, for examlple regarding to earnings.
- *Proposal 5:* We need to think over and decide what will be the truly important public purposes in Hungary and it is time to realize them.

CONCLUSION

Before the change of the regime it seemed that the reformers had a clear concept of the future society in Hungary and currently the circumstances are given to improve the economic position of Hungary and realize a modern, well-organized society which is founded on a democratic basis.

The statistics prove that in the last period the economy performed well, but there are visible signs of bust and the Hungarian economy and society are sensitive. The necessary tools are available but because of the lack of a sweeping structural reform, the results will be interimistic. Transmittance of a well-founded economy and society for the next generations is our colletive responsibility.

REFERENCES

[1] Hungarian Financial Supervisory Authority. 2019. *Annual Report 2006.* Accessed January 20. http://alk.mnb.hu/data/cms1290530/pszafen_annualreport_2006.pdf.

[2] Pénziránytű Alapítvány. "OECD Kutatási eredmények" *Money Compass Fund. Results of OECD survey* Accessed January 20. https://penziranytu.hu/magyar-lakossag-penzugyi-kulturaja.

[3] Magyar Nemzeti Bank. *Hungarian National Bank as the Central Bank of Hungary.* 2019. Report on financial stability update October 2008 Accessed January 20. https://www.mnb.hu/letoltes/overall-assessment-20081008.pdf.

[4] Hungarian Financial Supervisory Authority. 2019. *Annual Report 2006.* Accessed January 20. http://alk.mnb.hu/data/cms1290530/pszafen_annualreport_2006.pdf.

[5] Hungarian Financial Supervisory Authority. 2019. *Annual Report 2006.* Accessed January 20. http://alk.mnb.hu/data/cms1290531/pszafen_annual_2007.pdf.

[6] Magyar Nemzeti Bank. Hungarian National Bank as the Central Bank of Hungary. 2019. *Report on financial stability update October 2008* Accessed January 20. https://www.mnb.hu/letoltes/overall-assessment-20081008.pdf.

[7] *Reuters.* 2018. Payment of EU funds to Hungary could be delayed: Commission source. Accessed January 20. https://www.reuters.com/

article/us-eu-hungary-budget/payment-of-eu-funds-to-hungary-could-be-delayed-commission-source-idUSKCN1LZ2K9.

[8] European Commission. 2019. *Dealing with macroeconomic imbalances.* Accessed January 20. https://ec.europa.eu/info/business-economy-euro/economic-and-fiscal-policy-coordination/eu-economic -governance-monitoring-prevention-correction/macroeconomic-im balance-procedure/dealing-macroeconomic-imbalances_en.

[9] European Commission. 2019. *Alert Mechanism Report 2018.* Accessed January 20. https://ec.europa.eu/info/sites/info/files/ economy -finance/com-2017-771-en.pdf.

[10] *Financial Times.* 3 January 2019. Europe suffers from the sorry state of its banks. Accessed January 20. https://www.ft.com/content/497d 4d9e-0f3a-11e9-b2f2-f4c566a4fc5f.

[11] European Commission. 7 March 2018. *Country Report Hungary 2018* Accessed January 20. https://ec.europa.eu/info/sites/info/files/2018-european-semester-country-report-hungary-en.pdf.

[12] Rabobank Nederland Economic Research Department. 2008. *Countervailing power of cooperative banks 2008 (working paper).*

[13] Magyar Nemzeti Bank. Hungarian National Bank as the Central Bank of Hungary. 2019. *Financial Stability Council.* Accessed January 20. https://www.mnb.hu/en/financial-stability/financial-stability-council.

[14] KSH. November 2018. *További fontosabb adatok.* [Hungarian Central Statistical Office. *Additional relevant datas.*] Accessed January 20. http://www.ksh.hu/tovabbi_fontosabb_adatok.

[15] GKI. 18 December 2018. "Emelkedéssel zárta az évet a GKI konjunktúraindexe." *GKI Economic Research Co. "GKI's conjuncture index increased at the end of the year" Additional relevant datas".* Accessed January 20. https://www.gki.hu/wp-content/uploads/2018/12/GKI_konj_1812.pdf.

[16] European Commission. Autumn 2018. *Economic forecast for Hungary* Accessed January 20. https://ec.europa.eu/info/business-economy-euro/economic-performance-and-forecasts/economic-performance-country/hungary/economic-forecast-hungary_en.

INDEX

D

E

F

G

H

I

J

K

L

M

N

O

P

Paleoecology of Peatlands: Quaternary Climate Reconstruction from Hungary

Authors: Gusztáv Jakab, Pál Sümegi, Erzsébet Szurdoki

Series: Climate Change and its Causes, Effects and Prediction

Book Description: This new book discusses research in regard to the paleoecology of peatlands, with a particular emphasis placed on Hungary.

Softcover ISBN: 978-1-61728-220-1
Retail Price: $59

Germany: Background and U.S. Relations

Editor: Danielle M. Becker

Series: Global Political Studies

Book Description: This book provides an overview of Germany's political and economic background and relations with the United States.

Hardcover ISBN: 978-1-61761-888-8
Retail Price: $130

Bulgaria: Environmental, Social and Economic Challenges

Editor: Teodora Raya Danailov

Series: European Political, Economic, and Security Issues

Book Description: In this compilation, the authors aim to determine whether there was an association between contact with urban greenery and displaced aggression in young people in Bulgaria and, if so, whether nature experiences were a significant mediator of that association.

Softcover ISBN: 978-1-53614-280-8
Retail Price: $160

Lithuania: Political, Economic and Social Issues

Editor: Bronius Kazlauskas

Series: European Political, Economic, and Security Issues

Book Description: Lithuanian economic, political and social development should be assessed from a historical perspective because Lithuania regained its independence in 1990 when the Soviet Union collapsed. *Lithuania: Political, Economic and Social Issues* opens with an analysis of the three stages of political, economic and social development in the period of Lithuanian independence.

Softcover ISBN: 978-1-53614-278-5
Retail Price: $95